May all your days be filled
with Extra Hot Fudge!

Deanna
Galatians 5:22-23

Extra
HOT FUDGE
Please

Daily Devotions

DEANNA DAY YOUNG

WESTBOW
PRESS®
A DIVISION OF THOMAS NELSON
& ZONDERVAN

Scriptures taken from the Holy Bible, New International Version®, NIV®.
Copyright © 1973, 1978, 1984, 2011 by Biblica, Inc.™ Used by permission
of Zondervan. All rights reserved worldwide. www.zondervan.com The
"NIV" and "New International Version" are trademarks registered in
the United States Patent and Trademark Office by Biblica, Inc.™
All rights reserved.

WestBow Press books may be ordered through booksellers or by contacting:

WestBow Press
A Division of Thomas Nelson & Zondervan
1663 Liberty Drive
Bloomington, IN 47403
www.westbowpress.com
1 (866) 928-1240

ISBN: 978-1-5127-4254-1 (sc)
ISBN: 978-1-5127-4255-8 (hc)
ISBN: 978-1-5127-4253-4 (e)

Print information available on the last page.

Library of Congress Control Number: 2016907822

WestBow Press rev. date: 5/26/2016

Contents

EXTRA HOT FUDGE PLEASE

A collection of devotionals to:
Encourage you to be the best person you can be;
Encourage you to make a difference to someone every day;
Encourage you to find your passion in life;
Encourage you to seek God in all you do.

There are so many people to thank who have traveled along side me through this journey. First and foremost, I have to thank God for giving me this opportunity and opening the doors in His timing. I have grown so much in my spiritual walk while writing this book.

 Thank you to my husband, Roger, who has been my biggest cheerleader in my speaking and writing ministry. I could never have done this without your support and love over the past 28 years of marriage.

 Thank you to my daughters, Kiersten and Morgan, for always believing in me and helping me with editing.

 Thank you, Mom and Dad for your continuous support, love and encouragement throughout my life as you taught me to work hard, be persistent and finish every task I set out to do. You have been good Christian role models.

 A huge shout out to my dear friends and special church family for feeding me ideas to write about and who have always encouraged me to never give up!

 Thank you, Stephanie for giving me tough love and telling me to quit procrastinating.

 Thank you Larry Bob and Pam for choosing my title.

Thank you, Michelle, for countless hours of listening to me and getting me out and about to help get my creative juices flowing (even if it was to buy a new purse).

 Thank you to my high school journalism teacher, Mrs. Moorhead, for helping create in me the love of writing.

 Thank you, Carrie McNew for the awesome artwork you created for the book cover.

 Thank you, Melissa Hanley for taking my photo for the book. You did wonders with what you had to work with! Hahaha

 Thank you, Amy for helping me with editing and for all of your encouragement.

 Thank you to ALL who believed in me, gave me opportunities to speak to your organizations and allowed me the pure joy of bringing my writing into your life!

Extra Hot Fudge Please

I love ice cream! I love mint chocolate chip ice cream covered in hot fudge. I was at an ice cream shop the other day and asked for my mint chocolate chip ice cream sundae and whispered *"EXTRA HOT FUDGE PLEASE"* - as if whispering was going to take away some of the calories. Actually I just whispered so other people wouldn't know I was asking for EXTRA hot fudge!

Have you ever had a Hot Fudge Cake from Frisch's restaurant? Let me explain - it's a thin layer of chocolate cake topped with a square of vanilla ice cream topped with another layer of chocolate cake topped with hot fudge!! But sometimes they don't put near enough hot fudge on there for me. I have been known to whisper *"EXTRA HOT FUDGE PLEASE"* when ordering the delicious dessert.

I was thinking about how I love those already rich ice cream desserts and then to add just a little EXTRA HOT FUDGE sends it over the top! That's how we are with God's blessings. We have so much already. God gives us all that we need and a whole lot of what we want. But sometimes we say, "Lord, could we have just a little EXTRA HOT FUDGE?" "Could you give me just a few more blessings?" "Just one more thing?"

It's not wrong to ask God for things. He wants to know the desires of our heart! But we need to remember to appreciate all that He has given us. We need to appreciate the everyday blessings as well as the extras. Look around and count your blessings for just one minute. And then thank God for **all** of your blessings .... and for **EXTRA HOT FUDGE!**

2 Corinthians 9:15 - Thanks be to God for his indescribable gift.

Puzzle Pieces

Have you ever done a 500-piece puzzle? My mother-in-law used to do them all the time. She would leave the card table up in the family room all winter doing puzzles. My girls used to love doing puzzles with her. Once in a while though, kids would be crawling around and bump the table and some of the puzzle would fall off or come apart. It took a lot of time to put a puzzle together but only a few seconds to have it fall apart.

Sometimes in life it seems that we work so hard and then one event, one decision, one situation can make all the hard work fall apart. It seems like our world is crumbling around us.

But that may be God's way of fixing something that we didn't know was broken. Casting Crowns has a song titled *Just Be Held*. One line in the lyrics says, "Your world's not falling apart; it's falling into place."

The next time it seems your world is falling apart, ask God to show you how He is really just shaking everything up and allowing things to actually **fall into place** – just as He puts life's puzzle back together.

The Art of Letting Go

Holding tightly to a balloon so it didn't go up in the sky.

Wrapping the string around my wrist so the kite wouldn't fly away.

Staring out the window of my freshmen dorm when mom and dad left.

Watching Dad's chest puff up as he tried not to cry walking me down the aisle.

Driving slowly away from my daughter on her first day of kindergarten.

Feeling my heart skip a beat as I left my babies at college.

Crying for an hour driving back to Indiana after leaving my youngest in Colorado.

Hugging my husband's neck as he left for South Carolina.

Wiping tears for hours when Kadyn was sick.

Emptying the tissue box when my friend moved to California.

Leaving my church after 30 years.

Comforting my dear friend when Dale died.

Trying to breathe when Emily was killed.

Burying my mother-in-law.

Saying goodbye to my sister.

There is no Art of Letting Go. There is only the Art of Letting God.

Isaiah 41:13: "For I am the Lord, your God, who takes hold of your right hand and says to you, Do not fear, I will help you."

This, my friend, is the **only** true Art of Letting Go.

Good Enough

Sometimes we tend to do things part-way and consider it "good enough".

What does that mean? Good enough? Good enough for what? Good enough for who? Who determines "good enough"?

If a surgeon is operating on us, we wouldn't want him to say "that's good enough" during the procedure.

If I am paying someone to service my car, I would not be happy when I pick up the car if the attendant says "I think it's good enough".

I would be a little nervous if I am at the dental office, and the dentist "numbs me up" and says "I think that's good enough".

Yet when doing things ourselves, we sometimes get caught up in the "good enough" syndrome. But we should be people of excellence. People of integrity. People of honesty.

We want God to handle our situations with perfection - not just "good enough". We want people to give us their best - not just "good enough".

Today as you read this and go about your activities, look to be a person of integrity, honesty and excellence. God doesn't want "good enough". He wants your best. We aren't perfect, but we can give our best to the God who sent His son to DIE for us. I sure am glad God's plans are perfect and not just "good enough for who it's for"!

Do You Have a Two? Go Fish.

I think some days our lives are like a deck of cards. No two days are ever the same. Some days we feel like a **King** or **Queen**, and other days the **Joker** gets mixed in our lives and messes us up. There are days we may feel **black** and gloomy. Things don't go as planned or sinful thoughts and actions creep into our Christian life. Some days I feel like Paul in Romans 7:15 where he says "I do not understand what I do. For what I want to do I do not do, but what I hate I do."

There are days we may feel **red** – like blood red – when we have been wounded by people's words or actions.

There are days we work better in **pairs** and days we have a **full house** of chores and chaos. Some days our "deck of cards" has no rhyme or reason and feels like a mixed up mess.

But then God comes along and **shuffles** things up and allows us to see how He has put everything in its proper place. Romans 8:28 – And we know that in all things God works for the good of those who love him, who have been called according to His purpose.

We find the positive in being a **King** or a **Queen**. We wear the full armor of God to stand up against the **Joker**. We remember Jesus took his **red** blood and washed away our **black** sins. We remember that He gives us Christian friends and family to help us **pair** up against the evils of the world. And we thank Him for the **full house** of blessings He bestows on us every day.

I'm thankful for God's handy work in our **cards** of life and glad that we do not have to play against this world all alone – like a game of **solitaire** - but instead that we are on the side of a loving God who is the **Ace** that **trumps** all things!

Be Your Own Fruit Inspector

Don't you hate it when you buy a container of strawberries and you get home and the ones in the middle are rotten??? It seems, the packaging has the "not so good ones" in the middle and the better fruit placed on the outside– making it LOOK appealing when you purchase the container.

But what happens? The rotten ones in the middle start contaminating and rotting the good ones around it.

That's why we need to be inspectors of the fruits of the Spirit in our lives. We can't have hate in our heart and portray love to others. We may think we can fake it, but eventually the rotten fruit, the hate in the heart, will come out and ruin the outside fruit.

We need to inspect our heart and the fruit that we produce.

Galatians 5:22-23 talks about the fruits of the spirit: *But the fruit of the Spirit is love, joy, peace, patience, kindness, goodness, faithfulness, gentleness, and self-control. Against such things there is no law.*

Ask yourself – am I more _____ than last year? Fill in the blank with the fruits of the spirit. Am I more "patient" than I was last year? Am I more "loving" than I was last year? Am I more "joyful" than I was last year?

If you can't answer YES to those questions, then do a personal inventory and inspect your life and your heart. When the Holy Spirit lives to the fullest in your life, the fruits of the spirit will be evident.

So take a little time today and inspect your fruit. I hope it's ripe and very productive!

Those Traveling with No Baggage May Go Ahead and Board

Traveling by airplane is very common and usually time efficient in today's world. Most airlines charge for baggage these days but there is no charge for your first two checked bags if you fly with Southwest® Airlines.

When I hear the word "baggage" by itself though, it makes me think of negative things – like the "baggage someone carries around in their life."

Someone may carry around the baggage of *regrets* - wishing they would have done things differently in their lives.

Some people may carry around the baggage of *disappointment* - constantly thinking of the way things didn't turn out like they had hoped.

Some people may carry around the baggage of *unforgiveness* - holding on to grudges over something someone did that hurt them and refusing to forgive and move on.

I would challenge you today to think about what baggage you want to take on this journey through LIFE. You can only take the baggage that is free – the ones that give us the "free"dom in Christ.

I challenge you to leave the baggage at the cross that holds disappointment, unforgiveness, hurt and anger. God doesn't want you to take those on this journey. He wants you to be able to take only the things that don't weigh you down.

"Now everyone take your seats and put on the full armor of God. Please stow the Sword of the Spirit in the compartments of your heart. Place your Bible in the upright position. Turn off all negative devices. And be sure your belts of truth are securely fastened. We should be ready for our journey at any time."

Digging Deep Down For Joy

Psalm 90:14 says "Satisfy us in the morning with your unfailing love, that we may sing for joy and be glad all our days".

You can't help but smile when you see the word Joy. Joy is an emotion that is described in Merriam Webster as "a feeling of great happiness; success in doing, finding or getting something."

Everyone receives that feeling of Joy from different things. When our kids played sports we got such Joy from watching them play. Seeing the sun shine gives me Joy. Spending the day with friends brings me Joy. Riding my bike and swinging on my porch swing brings me Joy. We could go on and on about what things bring us Joy.

As I think about Joy, I think about these *things* that bring me Joy but knowing that God has given me all these things is what really brings me Joy. Sometimes Joy and Happiness are intertwined and considered the same thing. Both Joy and Happiness give us great feelings. But it is important to realize that Joy goes deeper than Happiness.

Happiness is a result of having Joy. Joy is deeper. Joy can be had even when we are not happy. Joy comes from knowing the Lord. Joy is a relationship with Jesus. Joy is a result of having God in your life.

Look inside you and see what brings you Happiness and then **dig deep down** and find your Joy – the Joy that only God can give! The Joy that is the fruit of having the Spirit living in you.

I pray you find great Joy as you journey through the day!

Phone A Friend... And So On And So On

I was laying in bed one morning thinking of all the things I wanted to get accomplished that day.

I got out of bed practically running to brush my teeth and get laundry in so that I could get everything accomplished on my mental list. I sat down to write out my list.

And then... I felt God gently put His hand on my shoulder and say "don't write Me on the list but start with Me. Don't work Me in your day, but start your day with Me."

So I stopped. Relaxed. Got out my Bible, and read. And one of the passages I read was in Proverbs 3:9-10 (NIV) – "Honor the Lord with your wealth, with the **firstfruits** of all your crops; then your barns will be filled to overflowing, and your vats will brim over with a new wine." Above that passage in my Bible I had written years ago "Put God first". I think this verse doesn't just mean with tithing. I think it means with time, talent, money and yes, Bible study on the busy days.

After I read that scripture and did my other readings, I felt the urge to share with other people what God placed on my heart that day. Maybe what He is telling me, and I am telling you, is exactly what He had in mind that day. You know, kind of like the telephone game? You start with something and tell a friend to pass it on to the next friend who passes it on to the next friend who passes it on and so on and so on.

Who knows all of the blessings we will see along the way by putting God first today and sharing with someone else what He did for us in the process? Then maybe they will share with someone else and so on and so on.

We Play Like We Practice

A quarterback was benched due to his lack of performance on the field. The backup quarterback became the starter. When asked about the reason for the change, the coach replied that it wasn't an easy change. He went on to say the original starter was very upset, but the coach was glad the quarterback was upset. He said, "this will make him work harder to get his position back".

Sometimes we play like we practice. If we don't practice hard and take it seriously, everyone can see the results of our lack of effort.

In the game of life, we must practice to be like Christ so we can be good witnesses for Him. If we don't read our Bible, pray regularly, attend worship, work on our relationship with Jesus and strive to live Christ-like, then our everyday life will be what we practice – no real connection to the Lord and a life that is lacking peace. But if we do those things then we will have a life full of blessings from the Lord and a peace that is hard to describe.

So ask yourself – what do I practice every day? Do I practice love, joy, peace, patience, kindness, goodness, faithfulness, gentleness and self-control? (Galatians 5:22-23). Or do I practice impatience, anger, hate and selfishness?

When we practice our Christian lifestyle each day, the fruits will be evident to those we come in contact with.

We need to remember that we want to be the best Christian we can be and if we do not practice the things that bring forth the fruits of the spirit, then we are practicing things that will make us a backup player. We don't want to be the backup. We want to be a valuable player on the team. We want to be a starter on God's team.

Now hand me the football… I'm ready to get started.

Be Contagious

When my oldest daughter was a toddler, there was an outbreak of the chicken pox virus, and we were careful to try and keep her away from the children who had the virus. Then we realized it was better just to give in and let her get the chicken pox when she was little because the health issues associated with getting chicken pox as an adult could be severe.

So we decided to let her play with the children who were already infected and she did get the virus and survived the chicken pox before age 5!! Why did she get them? Because they are highly contagious.

I don't recommend trying to contract contagious diseases. But what if we use this example to contract something positive that is contagious.

What if you could be the contagious one that people wanted to be around because of your positive attitude? Have you ever been around someone who seems to be happy all the time?

There are people who seem to find the good in any situation no matter what difficulty they may be going through. They live out Philippians 4:11(b) where Paul says "I have learned to be content whatever the circumstances". Paul had Joy in his life because of his salvation in Jesus Christ.

Being around people who have true Joy can be contagious. The love of the Lord shines through them, and it's contagious.

My challenge to you today is to show Joy to others. Keep spreading the joy like wild flowers in an open field! Be the seed that is planting Joy in others today!

Go on... Be contagious!!

There's An App For That

We have become a SMART PHONE world! Almost everyone you know has a smart phone. If you have a question, you can look it up on your smart phone. Anywhere. Anytime.

There are so many apps you can download to your phone so that everything is just a "touch" away. I asked my friend the other day if she knew what the price of gas was in town. She said, "there's an app for that."

I've come to realize that there is an "app" for about anything you want. I also realize that the more apps you have running on your phone, the quicker your battery runs down.

We are a lot like smart phones, aren't we? We keep adding more and more "apps" to our lives. We just keep running and going and doing more and more. Everything we do seems to be "good stuff" but we just keep piling on. We have too many apps running and we need recharged.

God is waiting right there for you everyday, every hour, every minute ready to help you recharge. He wants to help you remove some of the not-so-important apps from your life. When we focus on Him and what He has called us to do, then we can focus on the most important apps in our lives.

Just like the smart phones, we need to be recharged every day. Starting your day out with Bible reading and prayer is a great way to get recharged. Weekly worship services and small group Bible studies are good "rechargers" as well. I Thessalonians 5:17 says to pray continually. This means to be in an attitude of prayer all day long, seeking God's direction and to be mindful of His presence throughout the day. He is plugged in and waiting to recharge us.

As a matter of a fact............I think there's an app for that............ download it at www.Bible.com.

Take A Time Out

In the game of basketball, teams are given a certain amount of time outs they are permitted to take during the game. Coaches are usually very strategic about when to use their time outs. Some try to save them but you can't take them with you so might as well use them.

I have a friend who is a coach and I give him a hard time about not using his time outs. Sometimes I yell at him from the stands and tell him he needs to call a time out. I tell him that if I see he needs a time out, then HE NEEDS A TIME OUT! Hahahaha

What is the purpose of the time out? It is to be able to give your players a rest or to correct something that isn't going right or to reevaluate the original plan and make adjustments.

Just like a basketball time out, we all need time outs now and then to regroup and rest; reevaluate and rejuvenate. Have you taken time out to connect with the Lord lately? We should start our day out with him in prayer and quiet time. If our day gets hectic and we feel disconnected, then we need to take a time out.

Don't be afraid to use it. You get an unlimited amount and you're not penalized for taking time outs. Use them for rest and to correct what doesn't seem right. It's better to take them on your own than to have God telling you from the stands! I hear the whistle now – it's a full time out.

Matthew 28:11 – Come to me, all you who are weary and burdened and I will give you rest.

The Power of the Long Line

We are not a patient culture. We do not like waiting in lines. We seek drive-thru banks and restaurants. We seek express lines and curb side check-ins.

So why is it that if a long line has formed outside of the normal "lines" we are drawn to that area to see what is going on?

In grocery stores, lines form for free samples of food and drink.

When we go to Smokey Mountains in Tennessee and drive through the park looking for bears, we always speed up to where all the people are gathered to see if they have spotted a bear.

At ballgames and concerts, fans race to form lines to see if they can get a glimpse of their favorite player or celebrity and snatch an autograph. People camp out for days to get the next best electronic device.

We are nosey and want to know what we may be missing out on if we are not part of the long line.

Wouldn't it be great if we were as excited to go to church that we wanted to camp out for days ahead?

Wouldn't it be great to have lines of people wanting to talk to pastors and church clergy to see how they can get connected to the One who provides this joy?

The next time you see people lined up to meet their favorite celebrity or get the next best electronic gadget, remember that we should be living our life for the Lord in such a way that people line up to find out more about where they can get what we have.

It's the power of the long line – the one in which God should be the center.

Pin the Tail on the Donkey Devil

A picture of a donkey with no tail is taped to the wall. Participants are blindfolded and spun around and handed a paper tail. They walk disoriented towards where they believe the picture of the donkey is and try to get the paper tail placed as close to where the tail should be. The one placing the tail closest to the correct location is crowned the winner. The game of "Pin the Tail on the Donkey."

Being blindfolded obviously makes it difficult because the person can't keep their eye on the correct placement area. Then spinning the participant around and getting them disoriented adds to the difficulty of staying on task.

It's funny to watch the person stumble around and miss the target. Sometimes they get really close and other times they are so far off you wonder if they even remembered where the target was.

But in life, it's not funny when we take our eye off the target. The devil loves to be the one to blindfold us with lies and his deceitful ways. He loves to get us off course and tempt us with things that draw us farther away from the target.

The longer we listen to him, the more disoriented we get and lose sight of the target – the target of heaven and serving the Lord.

It's time we place a hard pin in the tail of the devil and send him off in the other direction. Remove the blindfold. Don't let him get you off track and dizzy.

Pin the tail on the devil and send him "hee hawing" in the other direction. Show him that you are staying on course and heaven bound!

No Passing Zone

When traveling on the highway we see all kinds of road signs. One of the most important ones to obey is the No Passing Zone sign. It is obviously designed to keep people from trying to pass other vehicles on the road at a location that could be dangerous.

Highway engineers know best and know exactly where to place these signs to keep travelers safe.

We should be aware of the No Passing Zone signs in our own lives. God has things in control but when He isn't moving fast enough for us, we tend to want to pass Him up and do things our own way. We are in a hurry and ignore the warning signs. We think we know best and sometimes decide to do it our way.

It's really best if we just heed the warning and let the Engineer on high tell us how fast to go and just let Him lead the way.

Jeremiah 29:11-13 – "For I know the plans I have for you," declares the Lord, "plans to prosper you and not to harm you, plans to give you hope and a future. Then you will call upon me and come and pray to me, and I will listen to you. You will seek me and find me when you seek me with all your heart."

Switch Me Seats

I love going on road trips with family and friends. I tend to drive when I go places with my friends. It's not because I don't trust them. It's just because I really like to drive and I guess that "control factor" takes over in me. When I drive, I can control the speed, the route, the stops, etc. Sometimes if I am the passenger, I get a little anxious if people aren't going the proper speed or paying attention to the road. There's that control factor again!!

If you are that way with the Lord and feel like you need to be in the driver's seat and control the ride, then you better switch seats. You've seen those signs that say "God is my co-pilot". I think it's much better if God is your pilot!

So as you go through this journey in life, just enjoy the ride and let the Driver lead the route, control the speed, and be in charge of the stops. If you find yourself trying to control the wheel, just ask the Lord to switch you seats!

Meet & Greet

I heard a comedian talking about how you could pay $2,000 to get great seats at a pop singer's concert which also included a backstage pass to a "Meet & Greet" event where you get to meet the singer and get autographs, photos and have a little chat with them.

The comedian said "why would anyone want to pay $2,000 to meet someone who doesn't want to meet them?" It made everyone laugh because as ridiculous as it sounds, people do it. We pay for the experience with a tiny bit of hope the celebrities will think we are awesome and want to be our friend!

Meet & Greet events are very surface. Yes, you get to enjoy the concerts up close and grab a few autographs, photos and maybe even a guitar pick. But the reality is that those celebrities probably won't remember you within 2 hours of meeting you.

But there is someone who has already paid the price for you to meet Him. He knows everything about you and will not forget you a couple hours after you meet Him. His name is Jesus. He is waiting to meet you right now.

It won't cost you $2,000 but it did cost Him His life. You won't get an autograph or a photo or a guitar pick but will you get a Spirit within you that will be with you forever.

You won't get His agent's cell number to keep in touch but you will get a direct line to talk to Him 24/7, 365 days a year.

Ask Him into your heart if you have not already. It will be the best Meet & Greet you could ever hope for. He's waiting... no pass required!

Reset

My husband's cell phone just stopped working the other day. He sent a text message and then picked it up and the screen was black. He put it on the charger for a while. Nothing. He tried holding the on/off button down. No luck. We tried everything we could think of.

Then we went to the technology brains of the family - our daughter! She said "oh you just have to hold this button at the same time you hold this button and it just resets itself". Wah lah!! The phone was working again good as new!

I'm so glad God gives us the opportunity to reset ourselves every day. All we have to do is ask for forgiveness and ask Him for direction.

No buttons. No black screen. No charger. Just a request, a repentance and a reset! Amen!

It Was Right There The Whole Time

Recently I feel like I have been losing my mind! I bought a special light bulb and when I got home I thought sure I had it in the kitchen. I looked the house over for that light bulb. I looked in the refrigerator, the freezer, the pantry and laundry room closet. I was thinking "did I take that light bulb with me somewhere and lay it down?" I even pulled the garbage bag out of the garbage can and searched through the garbage to look for that silly light bulb.

I decided to just give up. I couldn't find it. The next morning I got in the car and looked down and there on the floor board was that crazy light bulb!! It had been in the car the whole time!

I find myself doing the same thing with God. Do you ever get worried about something and start looking for the answers on your own? We try to fix things and recreate situations so that they are fixed the way we think they should be.

Then we look around and realize God was there the whole time. He was in the blessings we didn't realize were from Him. He was in the closed door that we didn't know was there to protect us. He was in the stillness of the morning and the song on the radio. He kept trying to show Himself to us but we missed Him in our search for other things.

We just need to be still and realize God is there... Just waiting patiently for us to see Him. Today, let's stop looking and just go to the One who knows all... the One who has been right there the whole time!

I've Got This!

Have you ever been with a friend, getting some popcorn at the theatre and he says, "I've got this." How nice for them to buy the popcorn for you!

Or you are getting ready to lift your groceries into the car and the bag boy says "I've got this" and lifts all your heavy bags of groceries into the car. That was sweet!

Or you're having lunch with a co-worker and the waiter brings the check and the co-worker says "I've got this." How very kind!

I will bet that your first reaction would be to say "No" and try to pay for or do it yourself.

Then you realize THEY WANT TO HELP YOU. They are doing the act of kindness because they WANT to do it. So you "let go" and let them have it!

That's how we are with God. We come upon a situation where we feel like we need to control the situation. But God gently places His hand on our shoulder and says "I've Got This!"

Our first reaction is to say "No. I can do it myself." And maybe we try and fail miserably. But God is still waiting right there saying, "please, let me have it. Seriously, I've got this."

He's already paid the price. He's already done the heavy lifting. Just let go. His way is better. Seriously.....HE'S GOT THIS!

Are You Wearing That Inside Out

A few years ago there was a young man who sat in front of me at church, and I noticed his shirt was inside out. The seams were showing clearly. The tag was staring me in the face. The colors were a little lighter from being turned inside out. It struck me very funny, and I had to try to contain myself from laughing out loud!

After the service, I politely mentioned to the young man that his shirt was inside out. He looked at it and said something like "Oh well, at least it looks the same from the inside out!" We had a good laugh out of it!

It makes me think about what if our "inside" was exposed. Would we look the same "inside out" as we do on the outside? If we were "inside out" would the world see a different heart and soul than the one we present each day?

I hope we all strive to have a clean mind, heart, and soul and that we aren't just presenting the good side to others and have a totally different inside.

Today... think about if you were "inside out". If you don't like what you see, ask God to help you clean it up so that you, too, can be like this young man and say "it looks the same from the inside out".

Bam... Debt Paid. Thank You And You're Welcome!

Credit Cards. We can use them at almost any place of business now. Fast food restaurants take credit cards. Every retail store takes credit cards. Even Redbox® movie kiosk takes credit cards. They are easy to use. They are handy to carry. No need to ever carry cash. Just one swipe and you can be on your way, merchandise in hand.

But then the mail comes. And buried in that stack of newspapers, magazines and junk mail are the white envelopes with the summary of spend for that month. Payment now due.

For some it's a good record to keep for all transactions and pay it off all at once.

For others, it's a reality of the accumulation of a bad "swiping" habit and immediate gratification that may take months or even years to pay off. Credit card companies are now required to put a chart on the bills that show how long it would take to pay off the current balance if you only paid the minimum payment each month and never added another spend to the balance. It shows the accumulated interest over that time period and how much it really costs you to use that card and not pay it off when the bill comes in.

The reality can be shocking. "How can I pay off this credit card?" What if someone came along and said I want to pay your credit card bill for you? Wouldn't that be awesome?!!! We may say something like, "you mean, I can keep all of the things I have but you will pay the debt?" And the answer is "yes. I will pay it all."

Well, folks - it happened. We get the joy of the blessings we receive every day. We get the hope for eternity in heaven no matter what all we have done wrong. We have someone who paid it all and He wants to give you this free gift of salvation and eternity in heaven.

Jesus paid it all. He forgives us. He wipes the slate clean! Accept God's gift. Live for Him every day knowing He paid the debt for all your sin. Giving your life to Him will be thank you enough!

Enough For Who?

The women of our church had a fun movie night watching "Mom's Night Out". If you haven't seen it, you should! It is hilarious. It's about 3 women who decide to have a night out and all the things that can go wrong with dads in charge of toddlers, preschoolers and teenagers.

One of my favorite parts of the movie is when the mother of three little ones is at her wit's end and has a chat with a new friend who is helping the women get these messes cleaned up. The new friend is a biker named Bones who is covered in tattoos with chains hanging from his belt. But he is a tender soul who helps the momma see that she is too hard on herself.

She is crying and feeling sorry for herself and saying how she tries to fix everything and just makes a mess out of it and she is just "not enough". And Bones asks her the most profound question: "Enough for Who? Enough for You?"

He is trying to get her to realize that she has set the standard for herself at perfection and when you try to be perfect, you will never be enough for yourself. But you need to be who God made you. You need to be YOU. You need to seek His will for your life and quit trying to be perfect and fix everything.

I think we all fall into this thinking at some time in our lives whether we are parents, coaches, bosses or friends. STOP IT RIGHT NOW! Stop feeling sorry for yourself. Stop worrying if you are "enough". You are enough!!

You go out and be who God created you to be. You love those kids. You clean that house. You coach that team. You lead those coworkers and you have fun and do things for your friends.

Enough for who? Maybe not enough for YOUR STANDARDS but you are a creation of God and He made you. You are ENOUGH! No Bones about it!

How Do Those Shoes Fit Ya?

I love shoes. The shoe section at Macy's® department store is my favorite. It feels like there are thousands of shoes displayed beautifully in a nice, neat little section that is so fun to browse.

I hate it though when I see those shoes on display that are gorgeous and they don't fit right. "Those would look perfect on my size 8 1/2 feet". The attendant brings the "Cinderella slipper" to me. I put it on and look down... and it's just not right. It crunches my toes together on the side... or it is way too tight... or it rubs up and down on my heel when I walk. I can't wear those shoes!

Did you ever think about where the saying "walk a mile in their shoes" came from? As a society, we love gossip. We can't wait to share the latest police blog or the latest tweet about a coworker who was spotted cheating on their spouse. We read internet posts to get the latest dirt on people to share with others. "It's just water cooler office talk" we say.

Ephesians 4:29 says "Do not let any unwholesome talk come out of your mouths but only what is helpful for building others up according to their needs, that it may benefit those who listen."

The next time you can't wait to share the news of someone else's drunk driving arrest or the neighbor's son being taken to the hospital for a drug overdose or even your coworker's sudden weight gain, STOP and think how you would feel if someone were gossiping about your life and your misfortunes.

Walk a mile in their shoes and see if they fit your feet like Cinderella's slipper or if you need to keep quiet and put those boots back on the shelf and walk quietly away... wearing your own shoes.

Let Your Flame Flicker Brightly

I love to burn candles. I love the little bit of light that it gives off in a dark room. I love the smell of a Christmas Cookie or Buttercream flavored candle. When I am ready to extinguish the candle, I just place the original glass lid on the candle and it smothers the flame.

Our lives are like candles. When we have the peace and love of Christ in our lives, we can light up the darkness of the world. We put off a "sweet smell" of kindness and joy to those we come in contact with. As long as we stay close to Christ, we can be a shining light throughout the world.

We must be careful not to let the darkness in this world extinguish our flame for Christ. We cannot let evil smother our joy. We have to keep the flame of Christian love burning brightly to light up our world - the rooms we enter; the places we go; the people we come in contact with; the world you are a part of.

Let God light the flame in your life and you keep it flickering brightly to light up the world you live in!!

Recharge Like a Bunny

My husband and I went on a mini-vacation over the weekend with some friends and spent several hours in the van getting there. At one point I chuckled to myself as I noticed 5 of the 6 of us were on our electronic devices. Thankfully the driver was not!

We had a Hotspot turned on the cell phone allowing the iPad® device to access the internet while traveling down the road for one of my friends to order her son's college books. Another friend was on her cell phone sharing some tips from a favorite internet blog, and I was thumbing through gift ideas on the Pinterest® website from my phone. It didn't take long for one of us to plug into the charger to recharge our device. All of that activity was causing our electronic devices to have the battery drained.

Those electronic device batteries are just like our lives. We have so much going on at one time that we can get the life sucked out of us pretty quickly.

Saying yes to too many things - even if they are doing for others and doing activities at church - can end up sucking the life out of us quickly. Work, kids, laundry, everyday chores, activities, church, fun and helping others are all good things. But don't forget to keep Christ at the center of it all. When you feel like things are getting you down and the world is spinning too fast, stop for a bit and get recharged by the One who gives Power and restores Life.

A little down time to RECHARGE is just what the body needs. Starting your day with a RECHARGE will make your battery last a lot longer. You may even turn into a little pink bunny with a drum!!

Staticky Radio

I was driving to work this week and trying to get my regular radio station, to come in on the radio. All I could get was static. So I changed to my other favorite station. More static. I chalked it up to driving the back roads and my location.

Sometimes it's that way with God. We pray but we just don't feel like He is listening. We have a hard time feeling close to Him. We read our Bible. We go to church. We do everything that we think we are supposed to do but it just seems that all we get is static.

Then we realize. It's our location! We have moved out of God's will, or we have strayed from the path of His direction. We realize we just can't hear Him clearly.

If you feel like God is far away, not listening or it's a little "staticky", then assess your location. Are you on the right path where God can come in loud and clear or have you strayed to the back roads and all you can get is static?

It's never too late. Just change direction, get on the right path and tune Him in. I bet His message will come in loud and clear and will be music to your ears!

Vending Machine Answers

I used to love vending machines growing up. We could put a quarter in there and push a corresponding button under the item and down it would fall for us to reach in and get our candy bar.

Then vending machines became more "sophisticated". Everything you could think of from toiletries to ice cream sandwiches were available in vending machines. Prices doubled and machines began accepting dollar bills. Numbers were placed under the item you wanted which corresponded to a keypad on the machine where you type in your selection number.

Sometimes we tend to look at prayers and God as vending machines. We send up a quick request and expect an immediate answer. We want to put the request in, type in the corresponding number and get the result.

Just like the selected candy bar, we want the result that we choose. Not the "your will be done" part.

We need to stop treating God like a vending machine. He's not always going to give us immediate answers or our requested selection. We've got to do our part. A relationship with Christ is required.

So this week, let's stop treating God like a vending machine looking for the THING we want immediately after we put in the request. Let's think about the ONE who can give us our request. His answers are much better quality than vending machine answers!

Full Custody

Divorce is a terrible thing for anyone to have to go through. Thankfully I haven't had to experience it myself. I have had to go through it with friends and I know that when children are involved it is very tough on the kids.

I read a book one time where the judge split custody of the kids between the parents but ordered the kids to live in the family home and the parents had to split their time between the family home and an apartment. If the kids were to be with a particular parent on Tuesday and Thursday and every other weekend, then the parent moved in and out of the family home where the kids were permanently staying. It was very hard on the parents moving here and there between the two locations.

Of course, this story had a happy ending and the parents realized how hard it was moving between locations and how much they missed each other. Their paths kept crossing by continuing to "live" in the same house and apartment and they reconciled before the finality of the divorce.

God realizes how much happier you are when you get to see Him everyday, too. He doesn't just want custody of you on Sundays and a day or two throughout the week. He knows how hard life is going to be each and every day and He wants to be a part of your day... all day, every day. Start your day out with Him. Talk to Him throughout the day - even if just a short talk now and then. And end your day with Him. It makes for a much easier life... full custody... every day... not just on Sundays.

Plan A vs. Plan B

I like a plan. I like to know where I'm going and where I will end up. Sometimes I even ask how a movie ends to decide whether or not I'm going to waste time watching it. I like to know the plan.

The problem with wanting to know the plan is that if the plan goes off course, it shakes me up a bit! However, believe it or not (even with what appears to an Obsessive Compulsive Disorder) I like spontaneity, too! So if Plan A doesn't work out, then I'm okay to go with Plan B. I like change and improvement - but I like to know why and where we're going with Plan B.

So you can imagine when my Plan A and my Plan B don't go as I imagined, that I start feeling a little uneasy and then need to figure out Plan C. But I'm learning through my Christian life that I can have a plan all the way to Plan Z and if God's plan is different, my plan doesn't matter.

God's plan will always win out. No matter how I try to control it and end up messing it up. His plan is better. His plan is bigger. His plan is more exciting. His plan is the best.

Ephesians 1:11(a) - In Him we were also chosen, having been predestined according to **the plan** of Him who works out everything in conformity with the purpose of his will.

So when you feel like things are just not going according to plan, then lay down the plan and pick up the cross!

Thriving in Ordinary Lives

We are ordinary people living ordinary lives. But is that what we are supposed to be doing? Living ordinary lives?

Casting Crowns has a song titled "Thrive". A few of the lyrics are: "We know we were made for so much more than ordinary lives. It's time for us to more than just survive. We were made to thrive!"

Our ordinary day may consist of the same routines. We may just be getting by. We may just be surviving. But God has made us for so much more. He doesn't want us to just "get by". Christians were made to do more. Christians were made to THRIVE and show non-Christians how awesome this "more than ordinary life" can be!

Give up the *ordinary* routine. Start your day with a daily devotional and some Bible reading. Ask God what He wants you to do today. Ask Him how each day can be just a little bit different. Ask Him how you can THRIVE!

Start today and do just one thing to move past "just surviving" and move into "THRIVING"!

REEEEEECalculating

If you have a GPS, then you know exactly what REEEEEEcalculating means!!

It can definitely be annoying because whenever you make a turn different from the one directed in the GPS, it recalculates. And it seems to get enjoyment out of barking the announcement of your mistake. "REEEEcalculating." And until you get back on the path drawn out in the electronic device, it will continue REEEEEEcalculating! It can drive you crazy!

But the device is leading you to your destination by the best possible route. If you have it set accurately, it will take you the shortest route and warn you of traffic or other delays. If you decide to take a different route, the car doesn't shut off or lock up. It simply allows you to keep going but continues to remind you that you are on the wrong path and will recalculate until you get back on the right path.

God is our GPS. If we can put our faith in God, we are putting it in the One who knows the proper direction. He knows the best route. He knows the shortest way and the pitfalls to avoid. But the problem is that we get off track and decide to take our own route and use our own directions and ignore His way.

He lets us go and doesn't "stop the car" but we do have to pay the consequences for choosing the wrong path. God does have to do a lot of recalculating in our lives to get us back on track. The good news is that if we will just listen to His directions, then our path will be easier and our destination worth the drive!

With God as our GPS, we will never be lost... just REEEEEEcalculated!

Hurry Up... And Wait

Hurry up and wait! That is how rush hour traffic feels. That is how Christmas shopping the day after Thanksgiving feels. That is how going into labor to have a baby feels.

Our lifestyle is based almost completely on time! We want to make the most of the 24-hours we have in a day. We want to make the most of the 7 days we have in a week. We want to make the most of the 30 or so days we have in a month. And we want to look back at New Year's Eve and see that we made the most of the last 12 months.

If things aren't going the way we want or in the time frame we want, we tend to take things into our own hands and get them "back on track".

How many times have you thought things weren't going the way they should be or in the time frame they should be, so you decided to take matters into your own hand and "fix them"? Did it turn out okay? Or did the matter turn out badly and you wish you wouldn't have tried to fix things?

God is in control of all things. Romans 8:28 (NIV) says "And we know that in all things God works for the good of those who love him......" Time is a protection. God knows we can't handle everything we think we can handle. Therefore, He allows time to be a protection for us.

Why don't you take off your watch, put *hurry* in the back seat and *wait* to see what God is going to do! It's gonna be awesome!

Splintered or Shaped? It's Your Choice.

Tongue depressors... you know the hard pieces of wood that doctors stick in your mouth to hold down your tongue so they can see your throat? You know, they just about make you gag because they are so stiff?!

Some people use these tongue depressors for a lot of craft ideas, too. I remember using the smaller versions of tongue depressors and making "log cabins" out of them when we were younger. We would try to bend them to make them go into a circle to make a swimming pool and every time, the stick would break as we tried to bend it - leaving me with a broken splintered little piece of wood.

It's like us trying to bend God's rules. We ignore the clear rules He has set out for us in the Bible and He allows us to break and splinter. His ways are best. He sees the whole picture. We need to let Him lead.

The tongue depressor CAN BE SHAPED if soaked in boiling water. It gets soft and you can shape it into a circle. It's just like us. If we soak ourselves in God's love and His word and ask Him to lead us in His ways, then He will shape us and mold us into the person HE wants us to be.

Quit trying to make God fit into your way and your rules. Let's soak in His word and His love and let HIM shape us. I would rather be molded into a circle by God, than be a broken, splintered piece of wood that can't be used to even flatten a tongue!

God's Memory Loss

Do you ever forget what you were doing? Or forget what you went into the kitchen for? You go back to where you came from just to remember what you were doing? Normal forgetfulness is aggravating. I think it also comes with age. (I'm not referring to the sad condition of Alzheimer's disease.) I'm just referring to everyday forgetfulness.

This is how God is with our sins when we ask for forgiveness. Psalm 103:12 - "as far as the east is from the west, so far has he removed our transgressions from us."

When we go to Him and ask forgiveness, He forgets our sins. It's like us going into the kitchen and just forget what we went in for. But if we don't accept His forgiveness and keep going back to Him with our sin, it's as if we don't accept His grace. It's like going back to where we came from so we can remember what we went in the kitchen for.

Don't go back to God with your sin. When we ask Him to forgive us, we need to forgive ourselves and accept His forgiveness. Don't feel like you have to "remind Him" how bad you were. He doesn't want reminded. He loves us so much that He has already forgotten and never to be remembered again.

The next time you forget what you went into the kitchen for, instead of getting angry, just whisper a little prayer to God thanking Him for His forgiveness and forgetfulness.

That's the greatest memory loss ever!!

Love Your Lamp

2 Samuel 22:29 - You are my lamp, O Lord; the Lord turns my darkness into light.

I love to decorate. I have my dining room and kitchen tables set all the time and decorated with different themes. I don't have the best china and silverware. Fun dishes from discount stores work for my themes. I love reading magazines and looking at Pinterest® for decorating ideas. My husband always knows when I've been diving into the decorating shows or books when he comes home to a mess and a smiling face saying, "honey what do you think about this idea?"

I love lamps, too. Not just any lamp - but really cool, unique, "turn-your-head" lamps. Something that can make a room POP! But as I was looking at some cool lamps and lamp shades recently, I was reminded that although the outside of these lamps are all different and fun, they all provide the same thing I need for that room...... LIGHT. No matter what shape or color of lamp I purchase, the result will be the same when I turn it on - a light to help guide me through the room in the darkness.

As Christians, we need to be portraying the light of Jesus. We are all made differently - different shapes, different sizes, different colors, and different styles but yet we all should give people we come in contact with the same thing - the light of Jesus.

Look around your house, find a lamp, turn it on and reflect on its glow. Then be inspired by that glow and light up your world today.........And maybe do a little extra decorating as well!!

TLC – Tender Loving Cards

I purchased a magazine the other day that has all kinds of cool cards to make. I love scrapbooking and card making and don't take time to do it as much as I would like. I thought to myself "I think I will start making a card each week and send it to someone special." I love getting cards and I love sending cards.

I looked at the front of the magazine and the title is "JUST CARDS!" I'm sure the meaning behind the name is "there are not any other kinds of crafts in this magazine - just cards."

But I wonder how many times we start to send a card to someone and then think to ourselves, "it's just a card. It doesn't really matter." But I'm telling you IT DOES MATTER.

In today's world of technology where the easiest thing to do is send an email and a text message, a card in the mail means a whole lot.

It means you were thinking of that person.

It means you took time to pick out a card.

It means you took time to fill it out.

It means you took time to look up the mailing address.

It means you took time to purchase a stamp.

It means you took time to stop and put it in the mailbox.

I challenge you today to send one card each week for the next month. It doesn't have to be homemade. Most every grocery store has cards. Just take the time to pick out an important person to send it to. Take time to choose the card carefully. Take time to write a few words. Take time to say a little prayer over the card before you send it asking God's blessings on the recipient.

They are not JUST CARDS... they are examples of a little extra touch of care. It's a TLC - tender loving card! And who knows... maybe you will get one in return. And I bet you will realize then - it's more than JUST A CARD!!

Identity Thief

In today's world of technology and credit cards, we see all kinds of tricksters hacking into electronic accounts and stealing people's identities. I have heard of people having false tax returns filed in their names; thousands of dollars charged on a stolen credit card within minutes; credit lines ruined in a matter of hours...........all due to sneaky, slimy thieves who spend more time being deceptive than trying to get a real job and do some good in this world.

That's the devil prowling around. He is stealing people's identities and being deceptive. He shows up in what seems like the coolest of places and the most exciting and fun things. He disguises himself and once he lures you in, sadness, depression, hurt and pain rear their ugly head and he is right there laughing in the background. He is the joker in the deck of cards. He is the murderer of dreams. He is the salt in the wound. He is the bottle to the alcoholic. He is the liar in the story. He is the villain in the fairy tale.

Be alert and of sober mind. Your enemy the devil prowls around like a roaring lion looking for someone to devour. I Peter 5:8.

Don't let him steal your joy. Don't let him steal your goodness. Don't let him steal your peace. Don't let him steal WHO you are. He is an identity thief and he wants nothing more than to be God. Don't let his disguise fool you. We protect our identity with one of the trusted protection companies. We should do the same with our Christian identity. God is the protection. His word the shield and answer to everything.

Just like you protect your credit cards and driver's license, hold tight to your identity in Christ. Be careful... the little thief is prowling around just waiting to strike!

Knock Knock... Who's There?

It's amazing how responsive we are to people who want to see or talk to us. Our cell phones ding at the sound of a text and we stop everything we are doing, including talking with a friend, to check our messages and respond.

We check email constantly having messages sent directly to our compact phones or our portable computer devices so that we are always able to access those requests and respond immediately.

We now have social media software that allows immediate messages to go out to millions of people to be tuned in to see what everyone has to say about everything.

We have capability to be able to connect by video to anyone at anytime.

If someone calls, we answer after the first ring because we can't stand to wait to see what someone has to tell us.

We cannot stand to make people wait when they beckon us. We want to know what they have to say or have to offer or what they need from us. We want to constantly stay connected. We want to respond immediately.

In Revelations 3:20, Jesus says "Here I am! I stand at the door and knock. If anyone hears my voice and opens the door. I will come in and eat with him, and he with me." Jesus is knocking at the door. He is calling for you. He has an offer you can't refuse. And it is eternity in heaven.

Why do we respond so quickly to those people in cyber land and people we don't even know? Jesus is standing at the door knocking, ringing the door bell, jumping up and down, and sending out all kinds of messages to get your attention. It's time to respond now. You cannot afford to put it off until tomorrow. Please make the decision to answer the door. Knock. Knock. Jesus Here.

Never Show Up Empty-Handed

I heard this saying the other day and it really stuck with me:
NEVER SHOW UP EMPTY- HANDED. Let's think about that...

1) Go to a friend's house for dinner - bring a covered dish.
2) Go to a co-worker's house for a party - bring a hostess gift.
3) Go to a meeting - bring a notebook and a pen.
4) Go to a wedding reception - bring a gift.
5) Go to a restaurant - bring your money.
6) Go on vacation - bring your camera.
7) Go to church - bring your Bible.
8) Go to an airport - bring your passport.
9) Go to a theatre production - bring your ticket.
10) Go to a doctor's office - bring your insurance card.

Almost every day we go somewhere and we always try to be prepared. We never want to show up empty-handed - without the things that we need. Each day when we enter the mission field of life, we need to be prepared as well. We need to be sure to study our Bible. Pray and seek direction from God. Ask Him where He wants us to go today. Ask Him who He wants us to help today so that we can be sure to be prepared and to never show up for God's work empty-handed.

Let's Have a Party!

There's nothing like a party to get your house in order! One year we had a family reunion at our house and we painted, did tons of yard work and house work just to get everything "so so". We wanted everything to be in tip-top shape when people came to visit. Anytime I decide to leave the laundry in the basket and not do the dishes after dinner, inevitably that's when we have house guests. I can have the house clean and organized and not a soul comes to visit but as soon as I decide not to pick up or run the sweeper, that's when unexpected guests arrive!!

I read one day that women really should not have their house spotless when they have guests over because it takes the pressure off of those who visit to not feel pressured to have their home spotless in order to invite you over. I like that concept. I want my home to be a relaxed and warm atmosphere where people are comfortable when they visit.

In our lives, we sometimes feel like we have to get our act together and make things perfect before we can ask Jesus into our lives. We feel like our "house" has to be in order and spotless for Him to come and live in our heart. But the truth is, Jesus doesn't want you to clean up your house and THEN invite Him in because it will NEVER be clean enough to your standards. Jesus wants you to invite Him in and THEN let HIM help you clean up your house - your heart.

For most of us, if we waited until everything in our house was spotless we would never invite anyone over and we would miss out on so much fellowship and fun. That's what Jesus says. Don't miss out on blessings and peace and hope and joy because you are trying to make your heart spotless. Just open the door and invite Him in. There's nothing like a party..........with the Holy Spirit........to get your house in order!

Fistful of Dandelions

I was thinking of dandelions as I was mowing one day. The yellow flowers can be such an annoyance as we attempt to create beautiful well-kept yards. We mow and the very next day they are rearing their little heads popping up one at a time until your yard is filled with those little yellow buds.

Each year my husband sprays our yard for dandelions so we only have a few weeks of the yellow flowers and then they become flower-shaped molds of white seeds that are shriveled creations in our yard. And obviously, eventually die out.

I remember when my girls were little, they would bring those yellow flowers by the fistfuls to me with their sweet little faces and dirty hands and proclaim with those big brown eyes, "I brought you some flowers, Mommy!" How many small jars full of those pesky dandelions did I have over the years!! But I cherish those times of my sink lined with those jars. I wouldn't trade the excitement on those little girls' faces for anything when they believed they had found a treasure.

After the dandelions had gone through their season of bloom, we would sit in the yard and pull up the white-seeded flowers and blow those little seeds to see how far they would fly.

I look at those dandelions like our lives. We can choose to focus on how annoying our problems are; how circumstances in our lives are not the way we wish they were; how we "fix" one problem and then another one pops up; OR we can look at our life situation and see the pretty "dandelion" as a gift from God. We can see the blessing in living through the trials until they fade away and we can blow the seeds of kindness into the wind and help others because of the trials we have overcome.

The next time you go through a trial or find something in your life that is just plain annoying, think about a sweet little pesky dandelion. They may crop up and ruin the look of your yard or your life, but in the end God is handing us a fistful of blessings.

Are You A Burned Out Light Bulb Or A Shining Star?

Have you ever been around people who seem to always have a complaint? It can be a perfect spring day but to them the sun is too bright or it's getting hot. They will be glad when cooler weather gets here. Then the fall and winter rolls around and they complain it's too cold and can't wait until spring and summer.

Some people can never say anything positive or find the good in any situation they have. They always have an "ache and pain". They never have enough time to get anything done. Their kids are always on their nerves and their spouse never does anything right. They are like a burned out light bulb - dark, aggravating and in need of some brightness!

My question today is "are YOU like the burned out light bulb? Have YOU ever been the one who complains all the time and can't find the good in the weather, the kids, the spouse, the house or your situation?"

I know sometimes I have fallen into the trap of looking at the negative instead of the positive. I begin to even annoy myself!! Philippians 2:14-16 says "Do everything without complaining or arguing, so that you may become blameless and pure, children of God without fault in a crooked and depraved generation, in which you shine like STARS in the universe as you hold out the word of life..."

Let's not be like burned out light bulbs complaining about everything. Instead let's be SHINING STARS IN THE UNIVERSE that light up those around us so that they can replace their burned out light bulb and go from dark to light. Become the North Star in your universe - you know.........the one everyone looks for and is easy to find because it shines so bright!

You Can't See Me

Have you ever played hide-n-seek with little kids? They hide in places where they can't see you and therefore, believe you can't see them! It's really sweet watching them feel like they are completely hidden because you are out of their sight. But, obviously, in reality we see everything they are doing.

As adults we tend to do the same thing. We think that God can't see the things we do when no one else can. We think because we are in the dark or alone that we are the only one who can see what we do. For example, you ask friends to hold you accountable to not eat sweets. And when you are home by yourself, you eat 3 cookies and don't tell anyone that you did it. Your friend didn't see you, and you were all alone so no one really knows that you ate the 3 cookies. But God knows.

People may think that God can't see them and doesn't know what they do because they can't see HIM! But think about the wind as an example. We can't see the wind. But we can see what the wind **does** and we can **feel** the wind. Therefore, we **believe** in the wind.

Look around... we can't see God. But we can see all the things He **does**. We can **feel** the Holy Spirit. We **believe** He is there even though we can't see Him.

So the next time you play hide-n-seek with God, remember that just because you can't see Him, doesn't mean He doesn't see you.

2 Corinthians 4:18 - So we fix our eyes not on what is seen, but on what is unseen. For what is seen is temporary, but what is unseen is eternal.

Who Are You?

Have you ever had someone come up to you and be so glad to see you and you have no clue who they are?

Oh, you try to fake it for a few minutes but finally the blank look on your face and the discomfort of continuing the conversation with someone you don't know overtakes the moment and you just have to ask, "WHO ARE YOU?"

Sometimes it is preceded by "I'm Sorry".........."I'm sorry but WHO ARE YOU?" It's embarrassing that you don't recognize them and that you have to ask. Or how embarrassing for the other person if they thought you were someone who you weren't and they have to say, "I'm sorry. I thought you were someone else."

We certainly don't want this scenario to repeat itself with Jesus. Get to know Him. Ask Him, "WHO ARE YOU?" and let Him show you. Read His word. Pray to Him. Live for Him.

Matthew 10:32-33 - Whoever acknowledges me before men, I will also acknowledge him before my Father in heaven. But whoever disowns me before men, I will disown him before my Father in heaven.

How wonderful to know if you have a relationship with Jesus that when you get to heaven He will never have to ask "WHO ARE YOU?"

VIP – Very Important Person

Several years ago I used to work with a production company who produced Country Music shows. I would drive artists and their staff to and from the hotels to the venues for their performances and do other errands requested by the production company. When I worked those shows, I always had a VIP pass to be able to have "all access".

I admit I was in awe of the celebrities and all that went into these productions. It was cool to be able to be considered a VIP and have access backstage. But after a while, I realized these people were just normal people like you and me. I realized that I wasn't really a VIP to those people. I didn't need to find my identity working backstage for a celebrity show.

I would come home to my husband and my two girls and realize I was a VIP to them no matter what I did - whether I was doing laundry, cleaning house, cooking dinner, playing Barbie® dolls or making cookies.

I realized I was already a Very Important Person (VIP) to the Almighty One. God had already stamped me permanently with a VIP tag because I was one of His. I would always be a VIP to Him.

So do NOT put your worth in WHO you are or HOW important you think you are. Put your worth in WHOSE you are.......you are a VIP of the King! All you need is a simple relationship with the One who paid the price for your eternity in heaven! Come on backstage with Jesus........no pass needed....you are already a VIP!!

Tape Measure

I was hanging something on the wall the other day that was a little odd shape. I measured the place where the nails would go on the back of the object. Then I measured the wall and divided that number in half, then subtracted one number from that number for the one nail hole and measured over to where the other nail hole would be. WHEW!! I thought because I had a TAPE MEASURE and was using what I learned in geometry and algebra classes, I was going to get that hanging just perfectly straight in the middle of the wall. I was so proud of myself... UNTIL I realized after it was hung that it wasn't exactly in the center of the wall.

Because of the odd shape of the hanging, I had measured the nail holes backwards because I had the hanging turned over while measuring the holes. How silly that was!! (I guess math wasn't really my strong suit!) I was so aggravated but I had already put the holes in the wall and decided I would just get creative and make it work by adding other decor on the wall and try to cover up the fact that the original hanging wasn't in the center of the wall like I had intended.

Aren't you glad God doesn't use a TAPE MEASURE to see if we measure up for eternity in heaven???

I can guarantee you that we would all be lopsided and crooked and not perfectly centered! But just like my decor on the wall to cover up my mistakes, God uses his grace, mercy and love to cover up our mistakes. The nails He used are ones that allow for our eternity.

Thank you, Lord that your TAPE MEASURE isn't like my yellow, gummed up tape measure that apparently I don't use very effectively. But instead that your TAPE MEASURE is covered with the blood of Christ and the grace and mercy to make us perfectly centered in your sight.

Quiet Please

Have you ever been to a golf tournament? As the golfer steps up to hit his golf ball, there are officials holding signs that say "Quiet Please". Spectators know that this is the protocol and when a golfer is getting ready to hit the ball, the crowd needs to keep quiet. The golfer needs complete silence to be in the moment.

When people are in movie theatres, notices on the screen remind people to turn off cell phones and to be quiet. People do not want to be distracted by noises as they watch the movie.

Why do they ask everyone to be Quiet in these situations? Because noise disrupts the golfer, the reader and the movie watcher!

It's the same when we have our Quiet Time with the Lord. He wants us to be in a place where we can focus on Him and His word as we read the Bible. He wants us to not be distracted by the noises of the TV, phones, and voices while we are spending time with Him. In order to do that we may have to get up early. We may have to go to the closet. We may have to go to the car.

Whenever you choose to have your Quiet Time with the Lord, it is important to focus on the QUIET part. Focus on the moment at hand. We may just hear Him whisper to us, "Quiet Please"...... reminding us to "Be still and know that [He is] God." Psalm 46:10.

Push One For More Prompts

Isn't it frustrating when you call a business and want to speak to a human being and get "Please Push one for a list of employees. Push two for Human Resources. Push three for Sales" and on and on. You get to number nine and it says "to repeat or to go back to the main menu Push nine". So you have to listen to all those prompts again just to remember what number you need to Push!!

Then you Push the number you think you need and get a second set of prompts: "Push one for a list of cars our employees drive. Push two for a list of food available in the vending machines. Push three for the colors available in the lobby area."

That's what it feels like... just give me a live person!! Sometimes it takes longer to get to the prompt with the information you need than it does to actually get the information!!

Aren't you glad we don't have to Push buttons to talk to the Lord! Can you imagine... "Push one if you read your Bible today. Push two if you have prayed in the last 24 hours. Push three if you attended church at least once this week. Push four if you did something kind for your neighbor. Push five if you need another chance." I think we would all have to Push five!!

The good news is when we call Him, He is right there. He is with us always. We may have to wait on our answer, but we don't have to wait to talk to Him. The next time you make a call and get a list of prompts, instead of getting frustrated, just be thankful this "prompt nonsense" is not God's way of life!

"Hello, God. Thanks for answering on the first ring."

Killing The Weeds of Worry

When spring approaches, we begin thinking about gardening. The biggest stress with gardening is the weeds. But when the weeds are gone, it is beautiful. We admire our flowers. We enjoy watching the plants produce the vegetables and the herbs flourish.

I think of our life as a Garden. God has given us this beautiful garden of life. He is there to take care of it for us but we keep filling it with weeds. Weeds of worry! We try to control situations because we worry God isn't going to handle it properly.

We worry what people think of us - how we dress, how we talk, how we think. We worry that what happened to someone else will happen to us. We worry that God will turn His back on us and stop loving us. It's time to get out the weed killer and KILL THE WEEDS OF WORRY!

God put Adam and Eve in the most beautiful garden ever. He gave them everything they wanted. There was no need for worry. And then Satan came into the picture. It is no different today. God has a beautiful life set up for us. He loves us. He forgives us. He is just waiting for us to trust Him. We need to have faith that He is what He says He is and that He is in control.

Worry and Faith are not compatible. It's time to put on the rubber gloves, get out the tools and KILL THE WEEDS OF WORRY! I guarantee you will enjoy your beautiful Garden of Faith!

Clothed With Compassion

If you are a female reading this you know how important the right clothes are - along with the right jewelry, scarf, purse and other accessories! If you are a male reading this, you probably just want to "be clothed" and it doesn't really matter what colors or styles you choose!

But whether you are clothed with the NECESSITIES or the ACCESSORIES, we all need to be clothed with compassion.

Paul wrote to the Colossians and told them as God's chosen people you are to clothe yourself with compassion, kindness, humility, gentleness and patience. (Colossians 3:12). To me all of these things go together because when you are compassionate, you are kind and gentle and patient and humble. Compassion is a great quality to possess. When you are compassionate, you show God's love to others with genuine care and concern.

Tomorrow when you get dressed for the day, whether you are putting on a suit and tie, sweatpants, a uniform, a dress or jeans, start by clothing yourself with compassion. (And then girls, make sure your purse matches your shoes.)

Following Footprints

I love seeing footprints in the freshly-fallen snow. The other day I realized we had a tiny little creature visiting us from the woods as I followed the rabbit footprints in the snow.

Footprints are created by footsteps that provide a path to a destination. I love when the kids were little and I would walk across the snow and then watch them try to follow me in the footprints. We even had Santa leave suet footprints on the ground one Christmas Eve so our girls could follow the footsteps to find their gifts on Christmas morning. When you don't know where to go, it's nice to have something to guide your footsteps.

The great news is that we have SOMEONE who has prepared the path for us in our lives. God has a big plan for us. Sometimes we get off course and our path doesn't follow His. But Paul tells us in Romans 8:28 that God uses all things for the good of those who love Him. Meaning that even if we get off course and suffer the consequences of our earthly decisions, God will find a way to use it for good as we go along the path of our lives. Nothing we do is wasted in God's plan - but suffering the earthly consequence of our ungodly decisions is much worse than if we would have stayed on the path and followed in HIS footsteps.

Put on your favorite shoes and get ready for the walk of your life - one footstep at a time.

Hear Me Roar!

Let's pretend for a moment that you are at the zoo. You see the lion is quietly sitting on the rock and looking around in all his arrogance. It seems as though you could walk up to him and pet that large, furry main. AND THEN ALL OF A SUDDEN he stands up and roars!!!

If you have ever experienced this kind of roar you know that sound ripples through you like a lightening bolt followed by loud thunder! And then I realize - I am at the zoo and the glass is between me and the lion. He cannot get to me to devour me.

Now pretend you are sitting on the grass near a wooded area watching the squirrels leap from tree to tree chasing each other. The deer are quietly eating the grass (or the farmer's beans!) and birds are chirping and singing. There is a gentleness with the squirrels as they leap, the deer as they graze, and the birds as they talk among themselves.

My friend, this is the way of the world. The devil is the roaring lion. He looks innocent enough and you believe you could walk right up and pet him. Then he roars! All of a sudden you are caught. He is chasing you. You feel as though he is going to devour you ....BUT THEN AS YOU RUN and scream for help, Jesus, the gentle One, reaches out His hand and pulls you to Him, saving you from the roaring lion and placing you back with the gentleness of the singing birds, the dancing deer and the playful squirrels.

I Peter 5:8-9(a) (NIV) says, "Be self-controlled and alert. Your enemy the devil prowls around like a roaring lion, looking for someone to devour. Resist him, standing firm in the faith..."

That lion is around you all the time, sitting in arrogance, appearing to just be a gentle pet. But when he chooses, he will roar and try to attack you. When you hear that terrifying roar and recognize the devil is prowling around, stand firm in your faith, because God the Almighty one is that glass between you and the devil - just like at the zoo. He will protect you if you ask Him to because He is gentle and kind. And when push comes to shove - He stands up on that rock, looks down on the lion and says "shut your mouth! Listen up! And Hear **ME** roar!"

No Leftovers

I don't like leftovers.

The other morning I opened up the refrigerator and found the leftover half of sausage stromboli I had the day before. I wrapped up the other half of the sandwich with good intentions to eat the rest at another time. But I'm just not big on leftovers. I think pizza warmed up is just too chewy. Pasta warmed up is too hard. If it didn't make the "first cut" then I'm not real excited about eating it the second day. The presentation is not as good warmed up as it was originally. The taste seems to be lacking for me.

But there is one leftover I like - DESSERTS. I can eat leftover pie, cake, cookies and cheesecake for DAYS until it's gone. A piece of leftover cheesecake or pumpkin roll is better on the second day. So I guess with the dessert theory in mind, I can't really lump it all together and say "I don't like leftovers". I just CHOOSE which leftovers I like.

But I can tell you right now that **God doesn't like leftovers at all**. He wants our best. He doesn't want what's left. He doesn't want yesterday's sausage stromboli or chicken pasta.

God wants the best. God deserves the best. Let's give Him our "firsts" and not our leftovers.

Proud As A Peacock

My girls always loved to have their Dad in the stands when they played basketball. They liked having me there, too but they REALLY liked having their Dad. We would always come home after the ballgames and highlight every important play and relive the excitement. They loved sharing these moments with their Dad and seeing how proud he was of them. They worked hard to be able to make him proud.

To this day I still like it when my Dad tells me how proud he is of me for something. I work hard and like to tell my Dad when I reach a goal or have success and secretly hope he is proud of me - even as old as I am.

We should work as hard for our Heavenly Father. We should spend each day:

1) studying our Bible to find out how to be more like Jesus
2) praying to God for direction in all of our decisions
3) spending time in worship honoring our Heavenly Father

Jesus lets us know how proud He is of us through blessings and the presence of the Holy Spirit sometimes found in that joyful feeling deep down inside. We also need to remember to tell those who look up to us how proud we are of them because it could open the door to share how we can work to make our Heavenly Father proud.

Who do you need to tell today that you are proud of them?

What do you need to do today to make your Heavenly Father proud of you?

Go on. Get busy. We've got a lot to do!!

Dented But Not Destroyed

A friend of mine had some bad luck with her car recently. She drives a VERY nice car. She ran into a wire and caused damage to one side of her car. Shortly after the incident and before she could get it repaired, someone backed into the other side! A friend of hers took the car to get BOTH sides repaired. He was driving home the "freshly fixed" car and hit a deer messing up the front of the car. Now that's a bad day!!! But she was a good sport about it all and is glad to have her car back all shiny and in good shape.

It reminds me of the Bible verse in 2 Corinthians 4:8-9 - "we are hard pressed on every side, but not crushed; perplexed, but not in despair; persecuted, but not abandoned; struck down, but not destroyed." We may feel like the sides of our lives are crushed in on the right, the left and the front and we have no way out. But do not give up or lose heart because Jesus died for us and God is reigning on the throne of this entire universe. 2 Corinthians 4:17 says, "For our light and momentary troubles are achieving for us an eternal glory that far outweighs them all."

Psalm 126:3, "The Lord has done great things for us, and we are filled with joy".

So as you go through the day and you get a dent, a bump or a scratch, just remember that Jesus is there with the tools to put you back in good shape with His Joy.

But you still probably need to watch out for the deer.

Oh The Tangled Lights We Weave

One winter I was putting Christmas lights on my bushes. I have those net lights and I try to keep them somewhat "untangled" during the year by hanging them from nails in the garage or attic to keep them straight. Well as I took them down and went to place them on the bushes, they got tangled and it was very frustrating trying to get them sorted out. Finally, I did get them untangled and got all of the shrubs covered with the net lighting.

Then the extension cords were tangled up as well. I was getting very frustrated with green extension cords. Finally I was able to get the lights connected, the extension cords plugged into the outlets and WAH LAH.......beautiful colorful Christmas lights!! The frustration was worth the end result of the decoration.

It reminds me of the difficulties in my life. Like when the lights are taken down, I find my life in order and planned and things stored away nice and neat and hung correctly so that no tangles occur. Then before I know it, I get caught up in sin and selfishness and find that I have made a tangled mess of things on my own. I tug and pull and try my way to get things to work and get untangled, when what I really need is a little patience and some assistance from the One who knows how to get me untangled.

When I focus on the Lord, I realize that no matter how big of a tangled mess I make of things, He is always right there to help me sort it out and make a beautiful creation of what was once a tangled mess.

When you get stressed or tangled, stop, take your time, pray, and get plugged into the power source - the Almighty God. Then........ You will shine BEAUTIFULLY!

Pennies from Heaven

How many times have you gone to the grocery store and the amount came up some dollar amount and 99 cents and you gave them the cash, they returned the penny and you put it in the "penny holder" by the cash register? Or you took the penny and threw it in the bottom of your purse or left it lay on the counter?

If we are walking down the street and see a penny we don't usually stop and pick it up, but if it was a quarter, we sprint to get it. We discard pennies in a jar because they are only worth one cent.

But how valuable is that one cent when our fast food order is $5.01 and we don't have any change? We sure wish we had that penny that we threw in the jar or in the discard dish at the grocery store.

It's a good thing God doesn't put those dollar values on us because we are all different. Some of us do small things like a penny; others do big things like a quarter. Some of us look polished like a silver dollar; others are more faded like a nickel that has exchanged hands many times over the years. But God sees the value in each of us. He doesn't discard us because we are small. God looks at the heart. He values every person the same - no matter how big or small, short or tall, male or female. He looks at every person as the most valuable coin in the piggy bank.

The next time you see a penny, think about how valuable it is. Think about how God values every person in this big piggy bank of a world. I think He may just send down pennies from heaven as our reminder at just the right time.

You're Not The Boss Of Me

When my daughter was little, my niece would babysit for her. It wasn't until years later that my niece told the story of how my daughter would tell her, "you're not the boss of me". My niece was a very good person to take that and not tattle on my daughter.

I can just see that little girl with those big brown eyes and sweet chunky little cheeks pointing her finger at the figure standing above her and smarting off with "you're not the boss of me" upon being told to do something she obviously did not want to do.

Although it was not a good attitude for my daughter to have toward her babysitter, we can certainly take that attitude toward the devil. When he gets in our thoughts and causes us to worry about things or tries to steer us off of our Christian walk, we need to point our finger at him and say "you're not the boss of me."

Colossians 3:23-24 tells us that the Lord is our boss. "Whatever you do, work at it with all your heart, as working for the Lord, not for human masters, since you know that you will receive an inheritance from the Lord as a reward. It is the Lord Christ you are serving."

Therefore, it is very accurate to tell the devil, the master of lies, that he is NOT the boss of you. Speak out loud and let him know who's boss... "Get away from me, devil. I work for the King of the universe! And YOU ARE NOT THE BOSS OF ME!"

Bowling Ball Battles

I went bowling the other day. We had a great time but I am really bad at bowling. I would get up to the line and with no skill or form at all, throw the bowling ball down the alley. Sometimes it would look like it was going straight down the lane and then veer to the left and end up in the gutter! Other times I would get a strike or a spare. I was very inconsistent.

I look at bowling sort of like life. The bowling ball is like the devil and we are like the pins. The ball comes in strong and knocks down the pins just like the devil comes in strong and knocks us to the ground. Then just like the big pinsetter comes down from the top of the lane and resets the pins, God comes down and wraps his arms around us, picks us up and sets us up again.

Sometimes the devil comes running after us and our spiritual strength gets him off course and he ends up in the gutter. We stand strong. The only way we can stand strong and resist the devil and send him into the gutter is to put on the armor of God which we find in Ephesians 6:14-17. Verse 11 says we should put on the armor of God so that we can take a stand against the devil's schemes - so we "bowling pins" can stand strong when the "bowling ball" comes right at us.

When we are fitted with all of this armor and standing in the bowling lane, no matter how fast the devil rolls down the lane to attack us, we will be ready to stand firm and veer the old devil into the gutter. If the devil knocks down our pins, God is waiting to come down as our pinsetter and set us upright and give us another chance.

Thank goodness for those pinsetters and gutters. I think I'm actually a better bowler than I thought!

All Aboard!

I love watching toy trains. I love watching the train go round and round a track especially if it's under a Christmas tree!! The sound of the "chug chug" of the train and the sparkle of tiny little lights glowing bring a smile to my face and a warmth to my heart.

It's so aggravating though when the train gets derailed and the normal roll of the train wheels is interrupted. But the good news is that when the train gets set upright again, it hugs the tracks and gets back in rhythm.

That's how our lives roll. We chug along enjoying the ride and all the sights and sounds along the path. Sometimes we get comfortable and something we do takes our eyes off of the right path and we get derailed. It may take a while for us to get back on the track and start rolling again. The good news is that we have Someone who can set us upright and put us back on the track.

Sin derails us. Forgiveness from God puts us back on track. I'm so glad to be on the train to heaven and even when it gets derailed by something I do because of taking my eyes off of the path, I am thankful for the ultimate Conductor to put the train back on the right track.

Won't you join me on this joyful ride? The seats are unlimited. The destination is to die for. Grab your coat and sit down. All Aboard!

Bite Your Tongue Until It's Numb

I recently had some dental work done and my tongue was numb. I could hardly talk and since it was such a chore to say anything, there were things that I would normally say or talk about that I decided were not important enough to put the effort into trying to talk with a numb tongue!

It made me think about the verse in the Bible, James 1:17, where we are told to keep a tight rein on our tongue.

We praise the Lord and sing praises on Sunday with the same tongue that on Monday morning criticizes our church family and spreads gossip about our friends. This cannot be! We must learn to keep a tight rein on our tongue. We cannot do this alone. We must have help from the Creator of the tongue!

Just like when my tongue was numb and I had to decide what was important enough to make the effort to say and what was not worth saying, we should be thinking that way all the time.

If you are convicted of how you use your tongue, I encourage you right now to seek help from the "dentist in heaven" who can numb you up and help you get a tight rein on that floppy muscle inside your cheek bones.

When you have something you want to say but know you shouldn't say it, don't just "bite your tongue" - go NUMB IT UP!

What's Your Giant?

You know the story of David and Goliath, the giant? David is a small shepherd boy but offers to go up against a Philistine man who is over nine feet tall and was a big bully! David hears the Israelite people talking among themselves about how big this guy is and how they are scared of these people. David explains to King Saul that he has gone up against lions and bears who have attacked his sheep and that God has delivered him from these animals safely and that he trusts God to deliver him from the giant in victory.

Saul agrees to let him go but he must wear a coat of armor, a helmet and a sword. But David wasn't used to all of this garb and told Saul he couldn't go out and fight the giant with all this stuff because he wasn't used to it. So he took 5 stones and a sling shot and went out to face the Philistine. After much mocking from the Philistine giant, David told him that the Lord Almighty, the God of Israel, was on David's side and the Lord will hand him over to David.

And as you probably already know, that is exactly what happened. David took out a stone and shot the nine foot giant man in the forehead and killed him.

What is your Giant? What is the nine-foot *thing* that you are afraid of and that just keeps mocking you?

What are you afraid to face? Is it a broken relationship that needs mending? Is it something physical that needs addressed like an unhealthy eating habit or weight loss? Or maybe it's an alcohol or drug addiction. Maybe God is calling you to do something that seems way too big for you to face.

Whatever it is today, I encourage you to pick up your stones, grab the hand of the One who can deliver you, and face your giant. It's time. You've been putting it off too long.

Pick up your slingshot, put in the stone, fire! Think about it. Pray about it. Identify it. Attack it. TODAY - Face your Giant. I know you, like David, can do it, with God's help and a little stone of faith!

The Excitement of An Elf

Have you ever seen the movie, *Elf*? There's a scene where the store manager announces to the employees that Santa is coming to Gimbles Department Store the following day and Buddy, the Elf, gets so excited. He jumps up and down and screams, "I know him! I know him!"

That night, Buddy hides in the store and after everyone is gone, he stays up all night and prepares the whole floor for the arrival of Santa by putting up lights, making elaborate decorations including hundreds of paper snowflakes and building a replica of the Empire State Building out of blocks. The whole floor is decorated to the max with Christmas décor.

It reminds me of when the kids were little and we would have everything just perfect for Santa's arrival - tree decorated and lit all night; gifts under the trees wrapped in paper that was left out for Santa to use; cookies and milk were left on the table for Santa's enjoyment; even reindeer food was scattered outside for the arrival of the big guy and his sleigh.

If only we would be that diligent about getting our "house in order" for the coming of the King.

If only we could get as excited about His coming.

If only we would be willing to jump up and down and tell everyone "we know Him"!

When the Christmas holiday rolls around, let's remember the baby Jesus and prepare our spiritual house for the coming of Christ and get as excited as good ole Buddy, the Elf... but scrap the green and yellow suit!

Living the Life of Royals

I was just thinking about the world's fascination with the British Royal Family. We watch every move they make. Tabloids report made-up information and "real media" report on the craziest of details - like what kind of jeans Kate Middleton is wearing to the park!

But we soak it all in. We want to read more and more about the Royal family to see when they will have their next child and what they name it. We want to see where they travel and what charities they support and the everyday people they help. We want to know where they get their clothes and if they are available to "normal" people.

I admit that I am fascinated with the British Royal family as well. I got up at 4 a.m. when I was in high school to watch Princess Diana come down the aisle with her magnificent wedding dress that included a 25-foot train.

But think about how much better this world would be if the media and the people around the world would put as much effort into reading and infatuation with being a part of the REAL ROYAL FAMILY- the one where Jesus is the King of Kings. It would be awesome if we were all as interested in reading about who He hung out with and the people that He helped. What if we could be as infatuated with His life and His every move and the miracles that He performed while on earth?

We don't have to rely upon media and tabloids to find out information about the real King. We have the Bible available that we know is the truth! There are stories upon stories of acts of charity and how He lived his life - even what He wore and who He hung out with.

We may not get media attention from our connection with the King, but I think it's pretty awesome that we are in line for the Royal kingdom and are already a part of the Royal family just for accepting the real King into our lives and trusting Him to lead us every day.

If you need me and I don't answer my cell, just leave me a message. I'll be having high tea with the King! You're welcome to join me.

You Look Just Like Your Father

I was teasing a friend the other day about how she acted just like her 90-year-old mother who she teases about being silly all the time. I said "you are your mother's daughter." The same evening we were visiting my husband's dad and I was reminded how much my husband and his dad look alike and thought "you are your father's son".

This made me think about Genesis 1:27 - So God created man in his own image, in the image of God he created him; male and female he created them. We are made in God's image. Somehow he has features combined by all gazillion of us on this earth.

As we live our lives, are we living the Christian life to show others that we were created in the image of our Heavenly Father? When someone meets us, can they say "You are your Father's daughter" or "You are your Father's son" meaning the Heavenly Father - meaning that they can see Jesus in the way we live our lives?

I want people to know by my actions that I am a daughter of the King. We need to work to show others what Jesus looks like by showing them love and kindness.

I'm not sure God has gray hair, double chin and dimples, but I do know I want to look like Him in the way I live my life. I want someone to say - "you are your Father's daughter." What can YOU do today to show you are a child of the King?

Hold My Hand

Have you ever experienced the soft touch of a baby wrapping their little hand around your finger? Their little hand is so small in comparison to just one of our fingers. Their soft, sweet hand fits so snuggly in the palm of our hand. It's amazing how the natural tendency of a baby is to grip their hand around your finger. I love that.

Isaiah 42 verse 6, it states: "I, the Lord, have called you in righteousness; I will take hold of your hand."

I just imagine God reaching down and grabbing my hand today as I go through the day. I wrap my hand around one of His fingers and realize the magnitude of the power of His hand holding mine. My hand fits snuggling into the palm of His nail- scarred hand. The roughness of His hand gives me comfort as I cling my fingers tight to the One who will lead me through this day.

If you find yourself struggling today with worry, fear, anger, jealousy or anything at all, just reach up and grab the hand that's stretched out waiting to be held.

These Feet Were Made For Walkin'

Have you ever looked at your feet and thought about just how important they are?

They hold you upright. The big toe on those feet keep you balanced. Our feet take a beating. We are on them a lot. When we carry anything of weight it adds to the stress on the feet. We pedal bikes with our feet. We stand, walk and run with our feet. Feet are important limbs to our body. Feet serve a purpose.

In Bible days, the feet were one of the most important forms of transportation. There were no trains, planes and cars. There were no bicycles, scooters and skateboards. The feet took a beating and were very dirty from walking the dirt roads everywhere one went.

Have you ever thought about how we could use our feet to do some of the same things that were accomplished in Bible days? We can use our feet to spread the gospel of Christ. We can use our feet to walk to our neighbor's house with food - "like five loaves and two fish". We can use our feet to walk down the hall of a hospital to visit a friend who is sick or "lower them through a roof for Jesus to heal". We can use our feet to make a difference to someone everyday just like the disciples did.

Pedicures and foot massages are great to make our feet feel better and look pretty, but past the appearance is a purpose. Think about how you can use your feet - on purpose - today to be more like Jesus. These feet aren't just a pretty "face"......they were made for walkin'!

The Little Culprit Who Changed My Plans

Job 9:27 – I will forget my complaint; I will change my expression and smile.

If anyone had reason to complain, Job did! He had lost his family, his home, his animals, everything in his life that mattered to him except his faith. Somehow he kept a good attitude and found a way to smile.

There are many days that things don't go exactly as I had planned. I like planning my day and feeling like at the end of it, I have accomplished a lot. If I can't see results, sometimes I complain and search for the culprit that interrupted my perfectly planned day of productivity.

But sometimes God has other things planned for me that are not on my to-do list. Sometimes the fruits of my labor may not seem like much to me in the "productive" mode that I like to be in. But if God decided to change my plans because His plans were better than mine, then I got accomplished exactly what He wanted me to accomplish – even if it wasn't on MY to-do list.

When things don't go as you have planned, forget the complaint, like Job did. It's not our circumstances that determine whether we have a good day or a bad day; it's our attitude about those circumstances.

I will remember today as I go about my day, with my to-do list in hand and my productivity mode in overdrive that I need to keep a good attitude even when things don't go as planned. At the end of the day, I hope I have a to-do list with everything marked off and a sense of accomplishment about me whether it was on my to-do list or the to-do list created by "the little culprit of change". And if the "culprit of change" happens to be God, then I will not complain because I'm pretty sure He is smiling holding His own scratched off to-do list!

Rest In The Nest

The other day I saw a nest of 3 baby birds. I got the binoculars out just so I could watch them. They were asleep for a while. Then they woke up chirping and opening their mouths because they were hungry. Pretty soon the momma bird came over with some worms to feed them. The momma bird seemed to stay around to protect them after they were awake until they settled down in a peaceful state again.

It reminded me of how we are a lot like those baby birds in our lives. We seem to be going through life peacefully and then some sort of problem comes our way and wakes us from that peace. We cry out to the Lord and he comes over with some spiritual food to help us. It's at this time when we need scripture reading, prayer and worship time to help get us through the tough times.

When we have been fed, we seem to go back to the peaceful state. But God stays right there with us to protect us. Just like the momma bird, He opens His wings to cover us during the storm. We snuggle up in His presence and allow Him to cover us with His mercy and goodness. When He thinks we have learned whatever it is He wants us to learn from the storm, then He allows us to go back out into the world. The only way we can live in peace in this world though is to continue to come back to the nest and live with His protective hand constantly covering us, thanking Him all the while for His protection.

Don't forget to come back home to the nest for a little rest.

Forrest Gump Had It Right

I was sitting on a bench outside of a restaurant waiting on my family. As I sat in the sun next to the American flag pole surrounded by colorful flowers and crisp green trees, I felt such a sense of peace. I have been praying for something specific in my life, and I just felt God tell me right there on that bench that I need to continue to have hope. Then a little butterfly flew right by me to rest on the flowering bush. One of God's small, simple, beautiful creations made me smile as I felt His presence flittering around me.

You see I've had a lot on my mind lately, and I've been praying a lot and haven't really seen the answers I want. And sometimes God doesn't give us the answers we want, but His plan is better than my plan. His ways are better than my ways. His thoughts are better than my thoughts.

"For my thoughts are not your thoughts, neither are your ways my ways," declares the Lord. Isaiah 55:8.

I know all that. I've read it. I've prayed it. But that day, God sat me on a little wooden bench in a flower garden outside of a restaurant and reminded me of it. Sitting on a bench. Waiting patiently. Taking in all the wonders around me that God put there. I think Forrest Gump was on to something!

Eenie-Meanie-Miney-Mo – Which Direction Should I Go?

Have you ever been hiking on trails and you come to a point in the trail where you have to make a choice? You can go one way, which may be labeled as longer or more challenging. Or you can choose to go a different way, which may be labeled less challenging and shorter. You get to choose the path you take.

Every day when we get out of bed, we get to choose the path we take, too. Am I going to be positive or negative? Is it going to be a good day or a bad day? The choice is ours.

What if we choose POSITIVE every day? Think about it:

Magnificent Monday.
Terrific Tuesday.
Wonderful Wednesday.
Thankful Thursday.
Fantastic Friday.
Super Saturday.
Splendid Sunday.
Thank goodness I have dishes to wash because it means I have food to eat.
Thank goodness I have clothes to iron because it means I have something to wear.
Thank goodness I have a car to wash because it means I have something to drive.
Thank goodness I have a floor to sweep because it means I have a house to live in.

We have choices to make each day. We can't always choose our circumstances but we can choose how we handle them.

I Thessalonians 5:16 says to be joyful always. That means in all circumstances. How do we do this? We can do this because our JOY comes from the Lord. It doesn't come from our children, our spouses, our jobs or our hobbies. Joy comes from the Lord and today, I choose Joy. Today I choose Positive. Don't be a negative ninny. Be a positive piper!

Eenie-Meanie-Miney-Mo – Which Direction Should I Go? Whichever one leads to positive joy. It's always a good choice.

Is It Really The Thought That Counts?

I've said and heard many people say before, "I meant to call you after your surgery and just got busy". Or "I meant to send you a card and just forgot." And then someone followed that up with "well it's the thought that counts".

I don't really think so....

Two years ago my friends threw me a surprise birthday party. It made me feel so special that my friends took time out of their day to come to a surprise luncheon for me!

As we were talking about how the event came about, one of my friends said, "we almost didn't do this. We didn't know how to get you here or who all to invite or what to eat and how to pull it all off. Then someone said, 'let's just do it.'"

After they told me that, I got to thinking about what if they would have just said, "we were going to throw you a birthday party, but we didn't know how to get you there; we weren't sure who to invite; we didn't know what to have to eat; so we just scrapped it. But it's the thought that counts".

That would have been so sad for me, but it made me think about how many times I have said something to someone and then said, "it's the thought that counts". But really it's not the **thought that counts**. It's the action that counts.

If everyone acted on the thoughts of kindness that came into our minds, think how awesome this world could be. Can we afford 10 minutes or 30 minutes to make someone feel special?

Think about what makes you happy. Do you like it when you get flowers? If so, send flowers to someone. Do you like it when you get a card? Then send someone a card. Do you like it when someone stops by for a visit? Then go visit someone.

Whenever someone or some act of kindness comes to your mind this week, act on it. It's really not the **thought** that counts... it's **acting out the thought** that really counts! Make a difference to someone ... today!

From Manna to Microwave – God Is Still The Same

I was making bacon in the microwave thinking about how thankful I was that I could have crispy bacon in about 3 minutes versus the way I used to have to make bacon taking 30-40 minutes, grease popping all over the stove and having to be a slave over the frying pan turning those fatty strips every little bit.

I was also thinking about smart phones and how we can get an answer to any question we have in a matter of seconds.

Popcorn has even changed. I remember my mom would get out the big pan and put oil in the bottom and put the popcorn in and shake that pan back and forth over the gas stove until the popcorn was popped. Now we can buy popcorn already popped and bagged or we can put a flat bag in the microwave and push a setting marked "popcorn" and have fluffy, buttery popcorn within a few minutes.

It is amazing how our society has changed over the years and now gives us quick satisfaction to our needs in a matter of seconds. Fortunately our God does not change like society does. He can't be put on speed dial or treated like "Siri" and expect immediate answers. The Bible says in Psalm 27:14 - "Wait for the Lord; be strong and take heart and wait for the Lord."

The Israelites had to wait on God. Job had to wait on God. There were many instances in the Bible of people waiting for God to answer prayers. We still wait on God to answer prayers today.

He's not a microwave. He's not Siri. He doesn't change like the latest and greatest in technology. We have to wait on Him today, just like people waited on Him in Bible times. And although I don't like to wait sometimes, I am sure glad that God is in control and knows all the answers. I'm glad His plan is better than my plan.

Thank you Lord for popcorn, bacon, Siri and answered prayers... yesterday, today and FOREVER.

It's As Easy As The Hokey Pokey

Psalm 47:1-2: "Clap your hands, all you nations; shout to God with cries of joy. How awesome is the Lord Most High, the great King over all the earth!!

Every morning we should get up clapping our hands and praising God for the joy of another day. We should be praising Him because he is the Lord Most High and He rules over all the earth!! If we get caught up in our every day troubles and all the trouble around the world, we will get depressed and may forget that we know the One who is in control! Keep our eyes on Jesus and nothing can take away our joy.

I know it sounds silly, especially if you are a Baptist or conservative Christian, but go to the woods outside all by yourself and clap your hands and shout to the Lord thanking Him for being in control. Tell Him how awesome He is!! It's as easy as the Hokey Pokey - put your right hand out. Then your left hand out. Put them together. Now shake it all about!!

Maybe you'll show up on You Tube! Just kidding!

The Ship Is Safe In The Harbor

The ship is safe in the harbor. But ships weren't meant to stay in the harbor.

We feel safe when we are in comfortable surroundings - like the ship in the harbor. We feel safe when we are at church. We feel safe when we are around our Christian friends. We feel safe in a routine. We feel safe with the familiar. But God didn't create us to stay safe in the harbor.

God created us to take risks so that we have to trust in Him. So that we realize we can't do it on our own. He wants us to take risks outside of our comfort zones. He wants us to trust Him to accomplish things for the kingdom we couldn't do on our own.

Being safe in the harbor makes me think of a boat tied to the dock and not able to go anywhere: safe; complacent; not moving far from the comfort of the harbor. We don't want to be like the ship in the harbor. God wants us to let go and let Him direct our path.

What does "letting go and letting God" even look like? It is a little scary. It will take patience, but it is a little exciting too! Not knowing where He will take us is exciting. We get so limited in our thinking when we are safe in the harbor. We just go through our every day lives doing the same things, eating the same food, wearing the same clothes, driving the same way to work and saying the same prayers.

What if today we cut the ropes loose from the dock and let the ship be steered by the Captain away from the harbor? Away from our "safe place". What if we took a chance - wind blowing through our hair? Spontaneous. Living in the moment. Letting Go and Letting God!

Get your hat ... we're going sailing!

Relax In The Rain

I was driving home in the storm and I could not see clearly at all. The lines on the road were invisible. The rain was pounding on my windshield. The wipers were washing as fast as the motor would allow, but they were not able to keep up. The road was flooding. The lightening was flashing all around me. It was getting dark, and I was getting nervous. As I approached the welcomed driveway to my home, I felt peace and comfort knowing I was pulling in the dry garage to waltz into my safe, dry living room out of the storm.

It reminds me of how I feel some days. I feel like the world is crashing down around me. I feel that I can't keep up with the pounding rain on my windshield. My mind is cloudy and nothing seems clear. I feel flooded with worries and troubles. The world and its easy fixes are flashing all around me, but I feel dark and alone and I get nervous and anxious.

Then I realize I must refocus on God and His "welcomed driveway" comes into view. I feel peace and comfort knowing that I am home in His arms and I do not have to be afraid. The storm will pass. The sun will come out again. And through it all, I realize God was in control all along.

God's Got This

There is no magic formula to not worrying. I think it is a very simple process but a very difficult process to implement. The process to me is every time you start to worry, you pray and turn it over to God. Sometimes I can do this and sometimes I cannot. But if we can't give it over to God, then we are saying to Him that we don't trust Him. We have to remember that He is in control of everything!!!

I read a story recently in my Bible study about a guy who decided to worry only on Wednesdays. So if something came to mind that he started worrying about, he wrote it on a piece of paper and put it in his "worry box." He didn't think about it again until Wednesday. On Wednesday when he went to review the items in the box and spend time worrying, he realized that a lot of those things had already taken care of themselves and he had forgotten about the issue.

I loved this story. Only instead of a worry box and going back to read over it on Wednesdays, I've tried to just give it up to the Lord when I start to worry. Sometimes I take it back and worry again and feel myself giving it back to Him - again.

Today... one day at a time... then tomorrow... just one day at a time... leave the worry at the foot of the cross. I saw a church sign that said "Don't Worry. God's Got This."

How simple. I think I'll go pray and then take a nap.

Peace In The Pasture

The other day I was driving to work down a side road and there were baby calves running and chasing each other, playing in the field. I stopped my car for a couple of minutes just to watch. They were so peaceful, carefree and happy. Not a worry in the world; running through the open field of newly greening grass and openness that seemed to go on for miles. I felt "peaceful, carefree and happy" as I watched them.

I got to thinking about how God smiles down on us when we give Him all our problems. When I lay all my problems at His feet and live life with joy and freedom, it glorifies Him. When God was talking to Moses in Exodus 33:14, He said "My Presence will go with you and I will give you rest." God's presence is with us and He wants to give us rest.

That's what I want today. That's what I want everyday. I want rest, peace and joy in my journey as I live everyday for Him.

Lord, as I go through the day and worries creep in my mind and negative thoughts begin to take over, help me to realize that you are the peace in the midst of the chaos. You are giving us freedom to run through the fields carefree and enjoy all the creation that you made for us to enjoy!

I hope you can find peace in the pasture!

Stock Market Advice for the Day - Relationship Business Has Biggest Return on Investment

If I asked you "Who matters most to you" what would you say? Your spouse? Your children? Your parents? Your friends? Do they know it? Do you show it?

Sometimes we live as if our relationships don't matter today because those people who matter most to us are always going to be there. We think we can take time to show them that we care sometime in the near future, but today we need to get extra hours in at work. Or we have Monday night football to watch.

Why do we wait until people are dead to send them flowers? Why don't we compliment others while they are alive instead of waiting to tell others how great someone was during a eulogy?

It seems that we SAY we value our relationships, but we don't take the time or energy to invest in them fully. Our busy lives and booked schedules take priority over our valued relationships and we end up taking for granted those that we love the most. People need to know that they are loved and appreciated.

Jesus told the disciples in John 13:34 to "love one another. As I have loved you, so you must love one another." He showed those He loved how much He loved them with the ultimate sacrifice. He is in the **relationship business**. He wants a relationship with each of us.

If you knew YOU only had a few days to live or the person who matters most to you only had a few days to live, what would you want that person to know? Tell them. Show them.

Relationships are important in our lives. Let's not take them for granted. We have a lot of everyday business to get done, but let's focus on our "relationship business". It has the most return on investment!

Have A Golden Day

Have you ever heard of the GOLDEN RULE? Do unto others as you would have them do to you? Sometimes people use that as a selfish verse when they want people to do something FOR them. But I think Jesus intended for it to be used to help OTHERS and then in turn to bless you for doing FOR OTHERS.

The verse known as the GOLDEN RULE is found in Matthew 7:12 - So in everything, do to others what you would have them do to you, for this sums up the Law and the Prophets. (NIV)

The Message Bible reads like this for Matthew 7:12 - Here is a simple, rule-of-thumb guide for behavior: Ask yourself what you want people to do for you, then grab the initiative and do it for *them*. Add up God's Law and Prophets and this is what you get.

I love the way the Message Bible translates this verse. **Ask yourself what you want people to do for you, then grab the initiative and <u>do it for them.</u>**

Do you like getting cards in the mail? Then ask God to show you who you can send a card to.

Do you like getting flowers? Then ask God who you should send flowers to.

Would you like for someone to make dinner for you one time? Then ask God to show you someone who is struggling in their life right now and go make dinner for them.

Doing for others will bring a smile to your face and sunshine to your day.

I hope you enjoy your big, beautiful GOLDEN sunshiny day!

Show the World Who's Boss

Do you ever wake up on a Monday morning and think "man I wish I didn't have to get up and go to work today?"

I was doing some studying in the book of Joshua recently. Talk about a guy who probably didn't want to get up and go to work!!

His co-workers were whiney.

He had a lot of responsibility getting those Israelites to the Promised Land.

He had to do a lot of traveling. His territory was huge. His workplace covered the desert from Lebanon, the great Euphrates river, to the Great Sea on the west; all the Hittite land. And who knows where else.

He didn't have GPS devices like we have now.

The work environment was hot and dry and sticky. I'm sure he got hungry and thirsty.

He was on his feet all day with no good insoles or ergonomically correct mats to stand on.

But he did have a Great Boss!! God led him all the way. He promised him in Joshua 1:5 "As I was with Moses, so I will be with you; I will never leave you nor forsake you."

God also encouraged him. "Be strong and courageous because you will lead these people to inherit the land I swore to their forefathers to give them."

The God of Joshua is the same God today. He encourages us to be strong and courageous in the workplace. He promises to never leave us nor forsake us.

We may work in an air-conditioned office or on a scorching hot rooftop.

We may drive around in a car or walk until our legs ache.

Our work space may be a 7x7 cubicle or a massive warehouse.

Our co-workers may be rude or they may be our best friends. Whatever the circumstances, God is telling us the same thing - "Be strong. Be courageous. I will never leave you. I will be with you wherever you go."

We can do it! We can get out of bed and be thankful for our work environment, our jobs, our work place and our co-workers because God is with us through it all. No matter if you work in a factory, an office, a school or at your home, today is the day to be courageous! Don't be ashamed of God.

Place a Bible verse in your work space. Lay your Bible in your office. Wear a piece of jewelry or something that shows your faith. Be kind. Be gentle. Be forgiving.

Show the world who's Boss... the King of Kings!

Be Patient And Keep Refueling

Have you ever been in a hurry to get to a destination and you are stopped by sudden traffic? I hate that. It seems that you are crawling at a snail's pace - or maybe the snail is crawling faster. A few years ago my husband and I were on our way home from a weekend trip in Gatlinburg, TN and we got caught in a 4-hour traffic jam from a semi trailer chemical spill. We were at almost a complete stand-still for 4 hours. People were running out of gas and pulling off the side of the road. Others were raising the hoods on their cars to allow some air to flow to cool down the engine. It was 4 lanes of traffic and no exit in sight. Nowhere to go. We just had to be patient and sit. Fortunately we had snacks, a cooler full of water, a tank full of gas and magazines to read.

Have you ever prayed for something over and over and just felt like you never could see an answer in sight? It's very frustrating.

As I was reflecting on some of my "repetitive" prayers that I have been praying for a long time, this traffic jam came to mind. There was nothing we could do except trust that the police officers and proper personnel would get the accident cleaned up as soon as they could. We couldn't do a thing to help. We couldn't go faster or change lanes or take an exit to get to our destination any sooner. We had to sit and wait.

Psalm 27:13-14 says: "I remain confident of this: I will see the goodness of the Lord in the land of the living. Wait for the Lord; be strong and take heart and wait for the Lord."

Just like when praying for something specific, we have to trust that God is doing the right thing in the right timing. No matter what we do, we can't make it go any faster. We have to sit and wait and continue to pray. We keep "refueling" through Bible reading, worship and additional prayer.

We just need to be patient, keep refueling and not give up. I am confident God's cleaning up the mess right now!

Get Ready For The Concert

Don't have your concert first and tune your instrument afterwards. - Hudson Taylor

In other words, don't get up and take off running into your busy day without some fine tuning first. We need to tune our thoughts and attitude towards God and godly things as soon as we get up in the morning. We need to start our day with quiet time in prayer and scripture reading.

Sometimes we go barreling head-first into the day with our own agenda, already hyperventilating for the day ahead and for the worries and hustle and bustle we have in front of us.

What if every day we started out with reading a daily devotional and a few passages of scripture and spent 5 minutes in prayer asking God for direction for the day?

I challenge you to do this for the next 10 days. I hope you will see the immediate difference and realize waking up just a few minutes earlier each day can give your day a fresh start and take away all those anxieties. God's already up and waiting for you.

Now go tune your instrument and get ready for the concert. It's going to be a lovely show!

Stop Looking in the Rear View Mirror

The past is the past. We all make mistakes and we will continue to make mistakes. That's the human side of us. We all sin. But we don't have to live with those past sins. We need to confess those sins and ask God to forgive us. And don't keep looking backwards!!

Don't keep reminding yourself of those past sins and certainly don't keep going to God asking again for forgiveness. He has already forgiven you and moved on. You need to forgive yourself and move on.

Paul tells us in Philippians 3:13 (B) that he is "forgetting the past and looking forward to what lies ahead." [New Living Translation]

When you are driving a vehicle down the road, you don't focus on the rear view mirror or you would get off track and wreck. No. You focus on the road before you and where you are going so you can stay on course.

That's how God wants us to live our lives - don't look in the rear view mirror at the past sins and get so focused on them that you lose direction to where you are going. Be like Paul and focus on what's ahead.

Got it? Are you ready? ... Ladies and Gentlemen - start your engines!!

Oh Those Fluffy Little Clouds

Have you ever taken time to just stare at the clouds? They seem to form shapes and figures for all to see. It's so fun to see what you can make out in the shapes. Sometimes we look so hard and create these little figures in our minds and truly believe that cloud looks like a particular thing, but someone else sees it differently.

One day I was looking at the clouds and clear as 20/20 vision I saw the shape of an alligator - teeth and all. When I showed my husband, he did not see it all. He said "I see what looks like a man fishing from a boat but I don't see an alligator."

A man fishing from a boat? How in the world did he get a man fishing from a boat instead of an alligator with mouth open wide showing its teeth? He was crazy and not seeing things clearly!

It makes me think of how we see our circumstances. I can look at a situation and create a scenario out of it that freaks me out. Someone else looks at my circumstances and may see humor in it. Someone may have been where I am and reassures me things will not be as bad as I have imagined in my mind.

Then we look at the situation through God's eyes and realize that He is using it for the good. We realize that when God is in control, all of those funny shapes and scenarios we think we see are really just "clouded thinking". Look through the eyes of the Son of God and realize that things are not as clouded as we think - just created, fluffy scenarios that God will control anyway - just like the clouds!!

Hope your day is full of Sonshine that overshadows any clouds!

Here, There and Yonder

When I was younger my grandma used to use that phrase a lot: "they are here, there and yonder." I may ask where my cousins were and she would answer, "here, there and yonder". We may chase the chickens around the barn lot and she way scold us telling us to stop because we were scattering them "here, there and yonder."

It seems to be a southern phrase such as "ya'll". But it's interesting that even though it may be deemed a southern phrase, we somehow all understand what it means. "Here, there and yonder" means something is HERE; something is over THERE; and something is spread all over the place [YONDER] - away from here.

That's how I see God's protection of us. He is with us wherever we go. We cannot go anywhere without Him. He knows all. He sees all. He loves us all. He is omnipresent. What does that even mean? Omnipresent. According to dictionary.com, omnipresent is defined as "present everywhere at the same time."

Well in this ole gal's understanding, that means God is with all of us all the time no matter where we are - here, there and yonder!

Place At The Table

Growing up we always had dinner at the table. Rarely do I remember us getting to use TV trays to eat in the living room. Mom almost always made a big meal and we ate together as a family around the table. As we got older and involved in activities, it became a little harder, but she always cooked and found time for us to gather as a family at the table.

My parents always encouraged more people to eat with us if they were there. I think there were a few times that our friends stopped by to "see us" but in reality were hoping to have a place at the table. Whether the dishes matched or not, there was always an extra plate to be had and an extra folding chair to fit around the table.

Being a part of family and taking time to share our day with each other around the dinner table was special. They are memories I still hold on to today and we tried hard to do that with our kids. I think everyone loves to have a place at the table to share laughs, stories and of course, food!

There is a table big enough for all of us in heaven. Jesus wants a relationship with us and that is all that is required to have a place at the table. Won't you call Him today and invite Him into your life.

Right now my dining room table is set with fun dishes and bright colors. It's time for dinner... grab you a place at the table.

It's As Easy As Flipping On The Switch

A few year's ago, we had a bad storm blow through our little town. I believe they even called it a hurricane. Power was shut down in some places for over a week. Our area was without power for 3 days. People were getting angry and frustrated because they needed their power source.

I don't know how many times I would go into a room and flip on the light switch - completely out of habit because I was so used to having power connected to that little switch. TV's wouldn't work. Refrigerators and freezers were turning warm. Boredom was setting in because we couldn't watch television and couldn't read very well by candlelight.

After several hours and realizing we may be without power for days, my husband decided to start up the old generator. We took extension cords and ran through the house to the TV, a lamp, the refrigerator and freezer and plugged into the newly fired-up power source. WALAH......power!!

It felt so good to have that source that could get us back to have some light in the house.... not to mention a little football on the tube! What is it that you are trying to do on your own today and you just can't do it because you are trying to create your own power source?

Give it up today and get plugged into the real power source. Jesus is sitting right there waiting to give you His power. He wants to be your Power Source. All you gotta do is go flip on the switch!

Slow Down. School Zone Approaching.

School Zones. Let's be honest... as we see those yellow flashing signs warning us to slow down in a school zone, we can become a little irritated - especially if it is the middle of the morning and we know the children are safe in the building and there is no bus traffic. We are so tempted to keep our cruise control set on 55 or 60 and just breeze on through the school zone.

When the speed limit changes to a mere crawl of 25 miles an hour, it seems that we could get out and walk faster. The slow zone seems to last for miles when in reality it is probably less than a half mile! It's good for us to have these reminders to slow down while going through an area where children are present.

God puts up these slow-down zones for us, too. We know we need to rest. We know we need to be going to church and praying more. We know we need to be studying His word more and acting in a gentler and kinder way. But for some reason we just keep on plowing through each day. We think we will start going to church more regularly when things slow down. We think we will just get through this crisis and then read our Bible more. We think we will just get through this stage in our life and then spend more time in prayer. We see the flashing warning signs but we don't slow down.

Psalm 46:10 says "Be still and know that I am God." This is serious, folks. Even more serious than a school zone speed limit. We have to stop and find time with our Creator. Heaven will not wait. God is patient to a certain point but He may also be tired of waiting.

School zone signs are designed to slow us down. How fast are you going? Do you get up and hit the road running? Are you on the cell phone constantly? Does your mind continue to plan for the next minute and never really focus on the conversation with your kids? Are you eating on the run and burning the candle at both ends?

Look around and see what signs God is putting in your path to get you to slow down and focus on Him. It's time to hit the brake. You are approaching the school zone. Slow down. Talk to Him. Read about Him. Visit Him.

Be... still... and ... know... that... HE... IS... GOD!

Bag The Rag Mags

Standing at the check out counter, we are tempted to read all of the "rag magazines" eager to tell us all of the gossip of the day. Some of the stories are absolutely outlandish. Celebrity A having lunch with an alien. Celebrity B having plastic surgery to make her mouth look like a horse. Celebrity C getting a divorce and cheating on his spouse that is just an absolute lie.

Celebrities sue these rag mags for false accusations and libel. We wonder why rag mags continue to print these lies when they know these things are false, but it sells magazines. It gets us to look and read and wonder if it could be true.

We spend hard-earned dollars and precious hours reading about these fake lives of celebrities, somehow wishing we could know them or be a part of their circle of friends.

When we get to heaven I am telling you that the Lord isn't going to ask you how many rag mags you read. He is not going to ask you whether it was true that Celebrity A had lunch with an alien.

But what He will want to know is whether you took time to read HIS piece of literature. Did we take time in our life to read the book that contains history, peace, advice and prayers? Did we take time to read the book that could help us live a better everyday life?

God wants us to bag the rag mags and spend time reading the truth. I challenge you today to read the Bible through in a year. It will take some time each day but you can do it. Just google "Read the Bible through in a year" and choose a plan that works for you.

I guarantee bagging the rag mags and reading the book of truth will keep your mind clear and give you something better to talk about at lunch... even if your friends do act like aliens!

Decisions... Decisions

What should I wear today?
What shoes look right with these pants?
Gold jewelry or silver jewelry?
Which way should I drive to work?
What should I have for breakfast?
Where should we eat lunch?
What can I fix for dinner?
What movie should I see?

Decisions.....decisions. We make a ton of them every day. Go on the yellow light or wait. Go 5 miles over the speed limit or under. Drive-thru or go in. Express line or regular check out.

We don't even realize how many decisions we have to make in a day. Sometimes we make good decisions. Sometimes not. Sometimes we don't think about the results until we suffer the consequences. Some decisions are bigger than others and some decisions have longer impact than others.

Whatever decisions you have to make today, I hope that you will choose to start your day with a devotional and prayer. Making the decision to take a few minutes and start your day with Jesus will be the best decision you make all day!

The Power of Multi-Tasking

I love the idea of multi-tasking. I am a list maker and the more I can get done and the quicker I can get it done, the happier I am. I love being productive and being able to accomplish more than one thing at a time. That is victory for the list makers of the world! I am so happy when my washer and dryer and dishwasher are all running at the same time and I am doing another task. Look at that... 4 things at the same time!! Mission accomplished! Productivity at work.

I realized this morning multi-tasking was at work first thing... I was doing my calf stretches while drinking my energy drink. I am backing up my phone while writing my blog. I was at the doctor's office yesterday and reading my book while waiting in the office - no need to just sit there. Be productive!

But this morning, while planning out my day off work to see how productive I can be, I realized that even though I start every morning out with Bible reading and prayer that lately I have been cutting my time with the Lord short. I am doing the task and marking it off my list, but not really spending quality time with Him. Praying in the car while driving to work is good from a multi-tasking perspective, but I'm not sure that's the only quiet time I am supposed to have with the Lord.

Multi-tasking is good when trying to accomplish a lot of chores and things on that to-do list. Productivity is good and it gets our adrenaline rushing to be able to see how much we accomplish. But multi-tasking with God is not the relationship He intended. When we multi-task, we have our minds on a lot of things at once. And although that could be considered successful to the "productive world", God wants our FULL attention.

Today as we go through the day and find ways to be the most productive and check the most things off of our to-do list, I pray that you and I will stop multi-tasking for just a little bit and "solo-task" our quiet time with the Lord. That down time of productivity will be the BEST time of productivity you will have all day!

The Masked Bandit Destroyed By The Hero

I was driving to work the other morning and on the side of the road trying to hide behind his cute, masked-bandit outfit was a little raccoon. Those creatures think they are so sneaky. We used to be bombarded by those pesky little creatures when we would camp. We would be sitting around the fire and raccoons were under our chairs and getting the marshmallows. One morning I looked out and saw raccoons had opened our cooler, removed the cottage cheese and ate every last little curd and left the plastic container behind. We thought we had everything secured. How did they get in the tightly closed cooler?!

They seem to be harmless, but they are actually very mean little creatures. They have sharp teeth, sharp little claws and will hiss at you if you get close to them. I've seen them do damage to a lot of things they wanted to destroy. They seem cute on the outside, but get too close to them or not keep things secure and they can do damage.

The raccoon acts a lot like the devil in our lives. He comes masked pretending to be something he is not. He waits patiently and works best in the dark of sin. He gets us to trust how cute he is and then he moves in for the kill. He gets us on his side and then seeks to destroy. He shows up when we least expect him - when we think we are protected from the enemy. He does his damage and then moves on to the next site.

Don't be caught off guard by the mask and the seemingly fun and cute ways of the devil. Once he gets his claws in you, he doesn't care if he hurts you or destroys you. John 10:10 (NIV) - The thief comes only to steal and kill and destroy; I have come that they may have life and have it to the full.

Reach out to the Savior instead of the Destroyer and enjoy the benefits of a life with Jesus. He is as real as it gets. No masks. No claws. No destruction. Just a life full of peace and protection. Move over you little masked bandit. You have been destroyed by the Real Hero!

Put A New Spin On Your Day

Have you ever had a toy spinning top? Some of you more "mature" readers may remember these. They are now called "retro"! I loved these tops. You pull on the lever and pump it getting the toy top to spin faster and faster. It's so fun pumping up the spinning mechanism and watching it twirl around with excitement!

But the spinning gradually slows down and eventually comes to a halt. I love Christmas and all the excitement around that time of year but Christmas time can be that way, too. We build up for weeks decorating, purchasing, wrapping, baking, cleaning and visiting with our family and friends as we are spinning with excitement and joy! Then it slows down and gradually comes to a halt. The Christmas-hype is over.

One of my favorite Hallmark movies is "It's The Most Wonderful Time Of The Year". Jennifer is just going through the motions of Christmas and says to her new friend, Morgan, "I will be glad when Christmas is over". Morgan, who loves Christmas and reminds Jennifer of her childhood excitement at Christmas, says "December 26 is the saddest day of the year".

We may feel that way, too. Work time off is either over or winding down. Kids are tired of new toys and dreading to go back to school. Schedules and "old normal" are rearing their ugly heads. For some, true depression starts to set in as the excitement of Christmas is over and the darkness of winter days appear.

But it doesn't have to be that way! We need to start each New Year with a **positive spin**. We too can be like the retro toy top! We can still be full of spinning excitement for EACH new day! When we understand the true meaning of Christmas, that Jesus came to earth for us, then we can truly live each day full of the spirit of Christmas.

Reality says that we cannot live pumped up like a fast spinning top every day. We will wind down and can't always be positive, but what we have available to us for the taking is the one that can fill us with His Spirit and get us full of the spinning excitement again.

I encourage you to think about the excitement of the toy top's spin. I want you to be filled with the spinning excitement of living each day with and for Jesus. And when December comes and goes and the commercial excitement of Christmas is over just like the winding down of the spinning top, we can keep it going by showing Christ's love to others all year-long.

We just need to keep pumping ourselves up with God's word, prayer, worship and daily encouragement. And when we feel ourselves winding down and falling flat, reach out to the One who can get you pumped up with excitement again. Let's vow to try and start each day with a **POSITIVE SPIN!**

Take It One Baby Step At A Time

My great-nephew is beginning to walk and he is so fun. He stands up and knows where he wants to go and starts to take off and falls down. In the last several months, he started with crawling. Then he would pull himself up. Then he would walk around things holding on. Then he would stand but didn't really know HOW to take steps. Then he learned to take one step, then two steps and pretty soon he was walking pretty steady by himself. He still stumbles now and then and likes for us to hold his hand as he wraps those sweet little fingers around mine.

It reminds me of our walk with Jesus. We know how we should act. We study it and sometimes we just can't get it right. We sin every day. But Jesus is right there holding out His hand to help us walk through this world; through these life experiences.

The more we walk through the difficulties of life, the stronger we get. The more we need Jesus, the more we reach for Him and hold His hand and wrap our fingers around His.

As you go through this Christian life, it's okay to start out taking baby steps. It's okay when you stumble and fall. Don't hesitate to take Jesus up on His offer to hold your hand. If you need Him, reach for Him. Don't try to go through this life on your own because YOU WILL stumble. You can't do it alone.

Some days we will just want to fall down and give up. But don't let the frustrations of this life allow you to quit. Just reach up and grab His hand and let Him lead you right through the day... one baby step at a time.

When is Enough Enough?

I really like the movie *Last Holiday* with Queen Latifah. It's about a gal who worked as a clerk in a retail store and lived in a very poor part of town. She was diagnosed with a terminal brain tumor and found out she had 3 weeks to live. She quit her job, cashed in all her stocks and bonds and went to live the life she had dreamed of living. She traveled to Prague and ran into the greedy CEO of her retail company but didn't tell him she worked for his company. Of course as the story goes, he learns from her and becomes a better person just as ... (wait for it)... she was misdiagnosed with a faulty CT Scan machine. She has met the love of her life in the meantime and opens a restaurant she had always dreamed of opening.

During the movie she says to the CEO, "when is enough enough?" and his response is "enough is never enough." But as the movie goes on he realizes money can't buy his happiness and he needs to change his attitude and the way he treats people. He realizes that whatever he has really is enough.

How many gifts are enough at Christmas time? How much money is enough to spend on each person on our list? When do we stop racing around and trying to keep up with what the world expects us to do? Cards, Christmas letters, gifts, cookies, fudge, parties, trees, lights, toys, gingerbread houses, concerts.

My question for you today is this: When is "enough enough" for us?

God sent His Son as the perfect gift. He was not born with trees and lights and gingerbread houses. He was born in a barn with cow poop, sheep slobber and smelly straw. It was enough. So if God sent Jesus into this world in this way and it was enough, then He is enough for us.

Keep your focus on the reason for the season and realize when enough is enough. Stop before it gets TOO MUCH. Trees, lights, gingerbread houses, cards, and gifts are all good things... but don't let that take over your Christmas. Don't get so exhausted that you don't enjoy the season. Remember no matter what you do or what you have, Jesus is ENOUGH!

Setbacks, Setups and Smiles

"What looked like a setback was really a setup for God to do something greater in Paul's life." - Excerpt from Joel Osteen's book *You Can. You Will. (c) 2014*

Do you ever feel like you are taking one step forward and two steps backward? You get the bills all caught up and then the car breaks down. You overcome a bad cold to then get the flu. You lose 5 pounds and then something stressful occurs and you snack away your sorrow! These are all setbacks. Some of them are in our control; some are not.

But no matter what - God is still in control - whether we are forging along and making great strides OR taking steps that make you feel like you have a setback.

Sometimes God uses our setbacks to wake us up and cause us to look to Him; to fall flat on our backs so we are looking up to the heavens; to surrender control and look to Him for strength. Don't look at what we refer to as SETBACKS in a negative way but rather look at them as SETUPS for God to do something great in our lives.

In Romans 8:28, Paul tells us everything is used by God for good for those who love Him. He has given us free will to make choices. If we choose wrong, he doesn't "control" that choice. We suffer consequences from wrong choices. However, God will work something good out of those bad choices so that He will be glorified in some way.

So the next time you have an urge to whine about the SETBACKS, make yourself stop, smile and think about how God is using those as SETUPS for greater things! You might as well smile...........He is!

Pride and Peace

In the novel and movie, *Pride and Prejudice*, we see the title portrayed by the attitudes of two characters, Elizabeth and Mr. Darcy. Both are very prideful and prejudice toward the other judging their upbringing and character as they clash personalities.

But as all good love stories go, the wall of pride falls down and they admit their love for each other. Throughout this story, there are instances of pride overtaking peace. They continued to argue and fight against each other when really they were striving for some of the same things and actually had a lot of the same ideals. But because of the initial feeling toward each other and not wanting to give in to being wrong, they continued on this prideful journey to almost lose an everlasting love.

I see this so much in our lives today. We are so prideful that we won't apologize or admit we were wrong about something. We won't admit we have more information or wisdom now and our thoughts have changed about something. I've seen pride break down families, tear up marriages, end friendships and cause people to turn against God. I've seen people give up eternity in heaven all because of pride.

Is there something that you are holding on to because you do not want to admit you may be wrong? Is there something standing in the way of finding peace with someone or maybe even peace with God because you can't let go of controlling something? Is God gently nudging you to put down your pride and exchange it for peace?

Whatever it is, I encourage you to lay down your pride and take the first step to peace. There is no greater love than this - that a man would lay down his life for a friend. (John 15:13) Jesus was that man. He died to overcome Pride in order for you to live in Peace. Pride goes before destruction, a haughty spirit before a fall - Proverbs 16:18.

Give in today. Give it TO HIM today. Lay down pride because I know Peace will feel much better than the hurt of the fall.

Sit, Soak and Sour

Have you ever been to a conference or a training session, sitting and soaking it all in - taking all kinds of notes and have great plans to implement the new ideas? You come back with a notebook full of ways to improve and ideas to try.

Maybe you read through recipes or get on Pinterest and find all these great ideas and you have soaked it all in with plans to do great things. You have a basketful of new recipes and so many "pins on the wall" you can't wait to get started!

Then a day goes by and you think "I will do that this weekend." Or "I will implement that new business idea at the start of the quarter".........then time goes by and all those great things you learned and superior plans to implement are still where you left them. It's like a gallon of milk that you purchase and don't use; it gets pushed to the back of the refrigerator and one day you find it and WOW!!! It's gone sour.

That's the way it is with us sometimes. We listen to pastors and speakers on Sunday mornings or Saturday evenings. We go to Christian conferences. We take notes; we make plans; we know what we need to change to live a better Christian life. We read our Bible daily and pray for direction. We have good intentions. But things get busy and we go back to our old familiar way of living and we become sour.

I encourage you today to look at your life and see what positive change ideas you have tucked away. What do you need to change today? What did you learn about God's plan for your life, the promises He has for you and what you can do for Him? What do you know but you haven't implemented yet? What are you waiting for? You can sit, soak and sour or you can sit, soak and SOAR! I want to sit at the feet of Jesus, soak it all in and then soar like an eagle ... I hope you do, too.

Isaiah 40:31 - But those who hope in the LORD will renew their strength. They will soar on wings like eagles; they will run and not grow weary, they will walk and not be faint.

The Trip Of A Lifetime

Going on a vacation is fun. We start by choosing our destination and then deciding whether to fly or drive, take a bus or a train. We choose our seat, buckle in and get set for the journey to our destination. We are looking forward to our trip!

Just like life. The Lord brings us into this world. We get to choose our destination for eternity - heaven or hell. Our life is really all about that journey. Some days we go by plane, car, bus or train. We put our lives in control of someone else besides us - the pilot, the bus driver, the train conductor. Even if we are driving our own vehicle, we are only in control of what we do and not what other drivers may do.

In life we really are not in control either. God is in control. We make choices and get to experience the results whether good or bad. We make decisions every day whether to choose God's way or the world's way. The journey is bumpy. We have good times, bad times, sad times and frustrating times. But through it all God is in control - leading the way to a beautiful destination. He wants us to enjoy the journey and has great things in store for us if we will follow Him.

I urge you to please choose heaven as your destiny. I ask you to let God be your pilot, conductor or driver. I beg you to seek Him on each decision every day so that you don't get off course and end up at the wrong destination. He is your guide. He is your compass. He is your GPS. Let Him lead. Choose Him. Buckle up. Seek His direction.

Be ready for a bumpy ride. But know if you choose heaven as your destination, and seek God as your cruise director, it will all be worth it. Eternity in heaven ... it's the greatest destination for the trip of a lifetime!

Let Me Introduce You To My Friend

When I was little, I had an imaginary friend. I talked to him constantly. I had a place at the table for him. He was with me when I played. I told mom and dad about him and made sure I introduced everyone to my friend. His name was Bobby.

Now, Bobby was a real person. He was my real friend. He was the son of my parent's best friends and we hung out a lot together. So he wasn't really "imaginary". He just wasn't physically with me all the time even though I pretended he was. He did have a place at my little table with the full plate/fork/cup setting even though he wasn't always "really" there to enjoy the pretend food.

It reminds me of my friend, Jesus. He is with me all the time even though I can't see Him. He is real and I talk to Him constantly. He is with me when I eat, when I walk, when I sit, when I sleep and when I am awake. I love spending time with Him and getting to know Him better. I love introducing Him to people. They can't see Him but I want them to know He is there. I want them to feel His love by my actions.

Bobby and I are all grown up now with families of our own and his name is now "Bob". Our parents are still friends. And even though Bobby and I don't eat together or play together anymore, we both know the same friend, Jesus and for that I am very thankful.

Friends are important and I hope you know our friend, Jesus, too. If not, I would be glad to introduce Him to you. Enjoy your friends, today! Maybe you can even take time right now to send them a note just to let them know you appreciate their friendship!

Light Up Your World

Have you ever flown on an airplane at night? When you are approaching the airport, the city is all lit up. I remember flying into Indianapolis one night and our plane took a small dip as it turned to one side to line up with the runway. I could see what seemed like the entire city lit up like a Christmas tree. It was beautiful!

Lights shine the prettiest when it is dark. I love sitting in the dark at Christmas time and looking at the lights on the tree, the mantel and the village all lit up. I love walking downtown in a city at night and just admiring the lights. At Disney World, one of the highlights of the evening is the light parade where dozens of floats glide by carrying characters that are decked out in costumes made of lights.

We are people who are just drawn to light. This world is full of darkness and sin. The devil loves darkness because evil is done in the dark. Darkness can be scary. But put some light in that darkness and evil begins to shudder because it is being exposed.

Matthew 5:14-16 says "You are the light of the world. A city on a hill cannot be hidden. Neither do people light a lamp and put it under a bowl. Instead they put it on its stand, and it gives light to everyone in the house. In the same way, let your light shine before men, that they may see your good deeds and praise your Father in Heaven."

How awesome it is that we can be the light in this dark world! As sin surrounds us and the devil tries to prowl around us in the darkness, we can show our light of Jesus to the world and light up the dark!

I thought my view was pretty from the airplane.......think about how beautiful the view is for Jesus........seeing His followers light up this earth.

Let's do it! Let's light up our corner of the world. Think how awesome this will be if we all just do our part! GO INTO THE WORLD AND SHINE BRIGHT!

** May God bless you as you continue your amazing journey through this life. And always remember along the way to ask for a little Extra Hot Fudge Please!